p. 42

p. 156 ksl pwra

p. 167 - structure

WITHDRAWN

Illinois Central College
Learning Resource Center

A Reader's Guide to Walt Whitman

a reader's guide to
WALT
WHITMAN

by Gay Wilson Allen, 1963

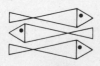

FARRAR, STRAUS & GIROUX • NEW YORK

Copyright © 1970 by Gay Wilson Allen
Library of Congress catalog card number: 71–97611
First printing, 1970
All rights reserved
Published simultaneously in Canada
by Doubleday Canada Ltd., Toronto
Designed by Betty Crumley
Printed in the United States of America

to EMORY HOLLOWAY who showed the way

Preface

In the early 1940s when I tried to find a publisher for a handbook on Walt Whitman, no commercial firm was interested. One, which had published handbooks on several major British authors, said it was ridiculous to think of publishing a handbook for an American poet. An amateur publisher, Walter Hendricks, accepted the manuscript for Packard and Company, then in Chicago. I am grateful to him for giving life to that work, but the distribution problems have been vexing. Five commercial publishers have inquired about bringing out a revised edition, but I have not been able to get my original contract revised, or to control the reprinting of the work, which has twice been reissued without corrections or revisions. This is the reason I have not kept the *Walt Whitman Handbook* up to date.

But even if the *Handbook* could be revised now, there would be problems. Every chapter not only is out of date, bibliographically and critically, but was written from the point of view of Whitman scholarship in the 1940 decade. Whitman was then well established in the academic world, but few major American poets or critics thought highly of him. All that changed a decade later, about the time of the celebration of the centennial of *Leaves of Grass* in 1955. The late Randall Jarrell probably did more than anyone else to rescue him from his misunderstood poetic reputation. Of course, not all of *Leaves of Grass* is now accepted as great poetry; in fact, critics have become more discriminating between the mediocre poems and Whitman's masterpieces.

In writing this Reader's Guide I have tried to give some idea of the enormous change in critical attitude toward Whitman, and some of the first critical reactions to *Leaves of Grass* are today both amusing and instructive. I have not attempted to give a condensed biography, but to indicate the more important biographical facts which help to explain the poems. On Whitman's literary theory and practice, a great deal more could be said—in fact, I have said a great deal elsewhere—but I have limited my discussion to what seemed to be most pertinent. If my preference for the term "Expressive Form" instead of the more familiar "Organic Form" is understood, I think it may prove helpful in appreciating the aesthetics and mechanics of Whitman's poems.

This book is intended as *an introduction* to intelligent reading and study of Whitman, not as an exhaustive analysis or definitive critical evaluation. I have particularly tried to indicate that the latter is still changing, and have summarized and commented upon the most recent attempts to interpret Whitman's poems in the contexts of Vedanticism, Existentialism, and psychoanalysis. So long as Whitman is read, critics will find new approaches to him; this is a test of his vitality. And he has never looked healthier than in this year of his sesquicentennial.

Oradell, N.J.   G. W. A.
May 1969

Contents

Chronology

1819 Born May 31 at West Hills, near Huntington, Long Island.

1823 May 27, Whitman family moves to Brooklyn.

1825–30 Attends public school in Brooklyn.

1830 Office boy for doctor, lawyer.

1830–34 Learns printing trade.

1835 Printer in New York City until great fire August 12.

1836–38 Summer of 1836, begins teaching at East Norwich, Long Island; by winter 1837–38 has taught at Hempstead, Babylon, Long Swamp, and Smithtown.

1838–39 Edits *Long Islander*, weekly newspaper, at Huntington.

1840–41 Autumn 1840, campaigns for Van Buren; then teaches school at Trimming Square, Woodbury, Dix Hills, and Whitestone.

1841 May, goes to New York City to work as printer in *New World* office; begins writing for *Democratic Review*.

1842 Spring, edits *Aurora*, daily newspaper, in New York City; edits *Evening Tatler* for short time.

1845–46 August, returns to Brooklyn, writes for Brooklyn *Evening Star* (daily) and *Long Island Star* (weekly) until March 1846.

1846–48 From March 1846 to January 1848, edits Brooklyn *Daily Eagle*; February 1848, goes to New Orleans to work on the *Crescent*; leaves May 27 and returns via Mississippi and Great Lakes.

1848–49 Ceptember 9, 1848, to September 11, 1849, edits Brooklyn *Freeman*, a "free soil" newspaper.

1850–54 Operates printing office and stationery store; does freelance journalism; builds and speculates in houses.

1855 Early July, *Leaves of Grass* is printed by Rome Brothers in Brooklyn; father dies July 11.

1856 Writes for *Life Illustrated*; publishes second edition of *Leaves of Grass* in summer and writes "The Eighteenth Presidency!"

1857–59 From spring of 1857 to about summer of 1859, edits the Brooklyn *Times*; unemployed, winter of 1859–60, frequents Pfaff's bohemian restaurant.

1860 March, goes to Boston to see third edition of *Leaves of Grass* through the press.

1861 April 12, Civil War begins; George Whitman enlists.

1862	December, goes to Fredericksburg, Virginia, scene of recent battle in which George was wounded; stays in camp two weeks.
1863	Remains in Washington, D.C., working part time in Army Paymaster's Office; visits soldiers in hospitals.
1864	Mid-June, returns to Brooklyn because of illness.
1865	January 24, appointed clerk in Department of Interior, returns to Washington; meets Peter Doyle; witnesses Lincoln's second inauguration; Lincoln assassinated April 14; May, *Drum-Taps* is printed; June 30, is discharged from position by Secretary James Harlan but re-employed next day in Attorney General's Office; autumn, prints *Drum-Taps and Sequel*, containing "When Lilacs Last in the Dooryard Bloom'd."
1866	William D. O'Connor publishes *The Good Gray Poet*.
1867	John Burroughs publishes *Notes on Walt Whitman as Poet and Person*; July 6, William Rossetti publishes article on Whitman's poetry in London *Chronicle*; "Democracy" (part of *Democratic Vistas*) published in December *Galaxy*.
1868	William Rossetti's *Poems of Walt Whitman* (selected and expurgated) published in England; "Personalism" (second part of *Democratic Vistas*) in May *Galaxy*; second issue of fourth edition of *Leaves of Grass* with *Drum-Taps and Sequel* added.
1869	Mrs. Anne Gilchrist reads Rossetti edition and falls in love with the poet.
1870	July, is very depressed for unknown reasons; prints fifth edition of *Leaves of Grass*, and *Democratic Vistas* and *Passage to India*, all dated 1871.
1871	September 3, Mrs. Gilchrist's first love letter; September 7, reads "After All Not to Create Only" at opening of American Institute Exhibit in New York City.
1872	June 26, reads "As a Strong Bird on Pinions Free" at Dartmouth College commencement.
1873	January 23, suffers paralytic stroke; mother dies May 23; unable to work, stays with brother George in Camden, New Jersey.
1874	"Song of the Redwood-Tree" and "Prayer of Columbus."
1875	Prepares Centennial edition of *Leaves of Grass* and *Two Rivulets* (dated 1876).
1876	Controversy in British and American press over America's neglect of Whitman; spring, begins recuperation at Stafford Farm, at Timber Creek; September, Mrs. Gilchrist arrives and rents house in Philadelphia.

1877	January 28, gives lecture on Tom Paine in Philadelphia; during summer gains strength by sun-bathing at Timber Creek.
1878	Spring, too weak to give projected Lincoln lecture; but in June visits J. H. Johnson and John Burroughs in New York.
1879	April 14, first lecture on Lincoln in New York; September, makes trip to Colorado, long visit with brother Jeff in St. Louis.
1880	January, returns to Camden; summer, visits Dr. R. M. Bucke in London, Ontario.
1881	April 15, gives Lincoln lecture in Boston; returns to Boston in late summer to read proof of *Leaves of Grass*, being published by James R. Osgood; poems receive final arrangement in this edition.
1882	Osgood ceases to distribute *Leaves of Grass* because District Attorney threatens prosecution unless the book is expurgated; publication is resumed by Rees Welsh in Philadelphia, who also publishes *Specimen Days and Collect*; both books transferred to David McKay, Philadelphia.
1883	Dr. Bucke publishes *Walt Whitman*, biography written with poet's co-operation.
1884	Buys house on Mickle Street, Camden, New Jersey. will not be "house-tied"; November 29, Mrs. Gilchrist dies.
1885	In poor health; friends buy a horse and phaeton so that the poet will not be "house-tied"; November 29, Mrs. Gilchrist dies.
1886	Gives Lincoln lecture in Philadelphia.
1887	Gives Lincoln lecture in New York; is sculptured by Sidney Morse, painted by Herbert Gilchrist, J. W. Alexander, Thomas Eakins.
1888	Horace Traubel raises funds for doctors and nurses; *November Boughs* printed; money sent from England.
1889	Last birthday dinner, proceedings published in *Camden's Compliments*.
1890	Writes angry letter to J. A. Symonds, dated August 19, denouncing Symonds' interpretation of "Calamus" poems; claims six illegitimate children.
1891	*Good-Bye My Fancy* is printed, and the final edition of *Leaves of Grass* (dated 1891–92).
1892	Dies March 26; buried in Harleigh Cemetery, Camden, New Jersey.

A Reader's Guide to Walt Whitman

I MAN OR BEAST?

What Centaur have we here, half man, half beast, neighing defiance to all the world?

—New York *Daily Times*, 1856

1

After a century of strangely contradictory abuse and worship, *Leaves of Grass* finally by the middle of the twentieth century attained almost universal acceptance as America's greatest single book of poems. Not all critics rank Walt Whitman as the first of American poets, but he is almost invariably named as one of the two or three best this country has produced—and frequently as *the* best. But for this very reason it is more difficult today to read Whitman's poems with the excitement they gave his first readers, who thought they were without precedent in literature. Someone has remarked that the greatest works of art have to create their own audiences, which is to say their own criterions for judgment; it is only the mediocre work of art that wins immediate acceptance—and then is usually soon forgotten. Of course, this observation is not always true, but many examples can be found in sculpture, painting, music, and literature to support it.

The curious thing about *Leaves of Grass* is that none of its early readers was indifferent. They either hated it or were fascinated by it (sometimes both at the same time), and either reviled or immoderately praised the poet. In this respect he was like the "revolutionary" leaders in American politics: Jefferson, Jackson, Lincoln, and the two Roosevelts, who were adored by their followers and irrationally hated by those opposed to their politics and actions. This was so true of Whitman in his lifetime that it is still difficult to get two critics to agree about him, even though they both admire his poems. Since no reader today can be entirely uninfluenced by Whitman's reputation, either as man or as poet, it is difficult to read his poems without some bias, to have a completely honest response to them. For this reason it is instructive to see the first edition of *Leaves of Grass* through the eyes of its first critics.

The book entitled *Leaves of Grass*, a thin quarto of ninety-five pages bound in green cloth elaborately embossed with flower designs, was first advertised for sale on July 6, 1855.[1] The title page bore no name either of author or of publisher but gave the place as Brooklyn, N.Y. In the technical sense, it had not been "published," having been printed at the author's own expense by friends of his in Brooklyn. The frontispiece was a well-executed steel engraving, made from a good daguerreotype photograph, of a young man with a short beard prematurely tinged with gray, wearing a heavy black hat slightly pushed back on his tilted head, posing in shirt sleeves, with shirt open at the collar, revealing the top of his red-flannel undershirt, his right hand resting on his hip and his left hand thrust into his work-jeans pocket. The posture was both nonchalantly informal and self-assured. This was evidently the author of the anonymous book (identified only on the copyright page as Walter Whitman). To understand how this frontispiece could shock anyone, it should be remembered that this was a period of formal dress (think of Lincoln only a few years later in his stovepipe hat and long-tailed coat) and dignified manners in literary circles: the "gentle" and gentlemanly Longfellow was America's favorite poet of this period—and one of Queen Victoria's favorites in England, too.

Putnam's Monthly, the leading literary magazine of the time, carried an anonymous review of *Leaves of Grass* in its September number. The reviewer, later revealed as Edward Everett Hale,[2] a Unitarian minister in Boston and future author of *Man Without a Country*, began:

> Our account of last month's literature would be incomplete without some notice of a curious and lawless collection of poems, called *Leaves of Grass*, and issued in a thin quarto without the name of the publisher or author. The poems, twelve in number, are neither in rhyme nor blank verse, but in a sort of excited prose broken into lines without any attempt at measure or regularity, and, as many readers will perhaps think, without any idea of sense or reason. The writer's scorn for the wonted usages of good writing extends to the vocabulary he adopts; words usually banished from polite society are here employed without reserve and with perfect indifference to their effect on the reader's mind; and not only is the book one not to be read aloud to a mixed audience, but the introduction of terms never before heard or seen, and of slang expressions, often renders an otherwise striking passage altogether laughable.[3]

The review then quotes from Whitman's preface to illustrate his theory of expression, which asserted: "Nothing is better than simplicity . . . To speak in literature, with the perfect rectitude and the insouciance of the movements of animals and the unimpeachableness of the sentiment of trees in the woods, is the flawless triumph of art." This theory of "simplicity" aroused mixed emotions in the reviewer:

> The application of these principles, and of many others equally peculiar which are expounded in a style equally oracular throughout the long preface,—is made *passim,* and often with comical success, in the poems themselves, which may briefly be described as a compound of the New England transcendentalism and New York rowdy. A fireman or omnibus driver, who had intelligence enough to absorb the speculations of that school of thought which culminated at Boston some fifteen or eighteen years ago, and resources of expression to put them forth again in a form of his own, with sufficient self-conceit and contempt for public taste to affront all usual propriety of diction, might have written this gross yet elevated, this superficial yet profound, this preposterous yet somehow fascinating book. As we say, it is a mixture of Yankee transcendentalism and New York rowdyism, and, what must be surprising to both these elements, they here seem to fuse and combine with the most perfect harmony. The vast and vague conceptions of the one, lost nothing of their quality in passing through the coarse and odd intellectual medium of the other, while there is an original perception of nature, a manly brawn, an epic directness in our new poet, which belong to no other adept of the transcendental school.[4]

In this second paragraph especially, the Reverend Mr. Hale shrewdly perceived Whitman's indebtedness to Emerson, which had yet not hampered his virile originality. The reviewer gives no indication that he is aware that Emerson had written the poet a few weeks earlier, congratulating him on "the most extraordinary piece of wit and wisdom that America has yet contributed." Emerson had found in it "courage of treatment" and "large perception," and greeted the poet "at the beginning of a great career, which yet must have had a long foreground somewhere, for such a start."

A second major review was published in the January number of the *North American Review*, a magazine of limited circulation but of considerable prestige in New England. Although the review was not signed, it was written by Charles Eliot Norton,[5] later to win fame as professor of art at Harvard and translator of Dante. We would expect him to be shocked by *Leaves of Grass*, and he was, but it was also, in Poe's phrase made famous by Edmund Wilson, "the shock of recognition":[6]

> Everything about the external arrangement of this book was odd and out of the way. The author printed it himself, and it seems to have been left to the winds of heaven to publish it. So it happened that we had not yet discovered it before our last number [the NAR was a quarterly], although we believe the sheets had then passed the press. It bears no publisher's name, and, if the reader goes to a bookstore for it, he may expect to be told at first, as we were, that there is no such book, and has not been. Nevertheless, there is such a book, and it is well worth going twice to the bookstore to buy it. Walt Whitman, an American—one of the roughs,—no sentimentalist,—no stander above men and women, or apart from them,—no more modest than immodest [see "Song of Myself," sec. 11] has tried to write down here, in a sort of prose poetry, a good deal of what he has seen, felt, and guessed at in a pilgrimage of some thirty-five years. He has a horror of conventional language of any kind.[7]

Norton then quotes Whitman's "theory of expression" from the Preface, and remarks that though other men have said this, "generally it is the introduction to something more artistic than ever,—more conventional and strained. . . . In this book, however, the prophecy is fairly fulfilled in the accomplishment":

". . . What I experience or portray shall go from my composition without a shred of composition. You shall stand by my side and look in the mirror with me. . . ."

So truly accomplished is this promise,—which anywhere else would be a flourish of trumpets,—that this quarto deserves its name. That is to say, one reads and enjoys the freshness, simplicity, and reality of what he reads . . . the book is a collection of observations, speculations, memories, and prophecies, clad in the simplest, truest, and often the most nervous English,—in the midst of which the reader comes upon something as much out of place as a piece of rotten wood would be among leaves of grass in the meadow, if the meadow had no object but to furnish a child's couch . . .

For the purpose of showing that he is above every conventionalism, Mr. Whitman puts into the book one or two lines which he would not address to a woman nor to a company of men. There is not anything, perhaps, which modern usage would stamp as more indelicate than are some passages in Homer. There is not a word in it meant to attract readers by its grossness, as there is in half the literature of the last century, which holds its place unchallenged on the tables of our drawing-rooms. For all that, it is a pity that a book where everything else is natural should go out of the way to avoid the suspicion of being prudish.[8]

Though Charles Eliot Norton is too refined to say so, he is disturbed by the frankly sexual references and descriptions in the book, for one of Whitman's major themes was that sex is pure and wholesome because it is natural. That there may have been secret causes for Whitman's passionate desire to defend

sexuality need not concern us at the moment; the important
point is that educated and refined men like Charles Eliot
Norton and Edward Everett Hale (Emerson too, as later developed) were irresistibly attracted by the vividness, originality,
and power of Whitman's literary expression in his first edition
of *Leaves of Grass*, but they *did wish* the poet had not so bla-
tantly made himself the medium of "forbidden voices":

> Voices of sexes and lusts . . . . voices veiled, and
>   I remove the veil,
> Voices indecent by me clarified and transfigured.
>
> I do not press my finger across my mouth,
> I keep as delicate around the bowels as around
>   the head and heart,
> Copulation is no more rank to me than death is.
>
> I believe in the flesh and the appetites,
> Seeing hearing and feeling are miracles, and each
>   part and tag of me is a miracle.
>
> Divine am I inside and out, and I make holy whatever
>   I touch or am touched from;
> The scent of these arm-pits is aroma finer than prayer,
> This head is more than churches or bibles or creeds.
>
> If I worship any particular thing it shall be some
>   of the spread of my body;
> Translucent mould of me it shall be you,
> Shaded ledges and rests, firm masculine coulter,
>   it shall be you,
> Whatever goes to the tilth of me it shall be you,
> You my rich blood, your milky stream pale strippings
>   of my life;
> Breast that presses against other breasts it shall be you,

My brain it shall be your occult convolutions,
Root of washed sweet-flag, timorous pond-snipe, nest of
    guarded duplicate eggs, it shall be you,
Mixed tussled hay of head and beard and brawn it shall be you,
Trickling sap of maple, fibre of manly wheat, it shall be you;

    .   .   .   .   .

I dote on myself . . . . there is that lot of me, and all so luscious,
Each moment and whatever happens thrills me with joy.

Naturally, the most bitter condemnation of such poetry as this came from the religious press and pious orthodoxy. Conservative minds thought Whitman's language was obscene, though he did not use the taboo four-letter words. He did, of course, use obvious metaphors for semen and sex organs, flaunting them as more sacred than bibles and creeds. His critics were sure he was a sensualist, a hedonist, and probably an atheist!

By the time the second edition appeared in 1856, augmented by thirty-two poems, the unsavory reputation of *Leaves of Grass* had received wide circulation. *The Christian Examiner*, supported by the more orthodox Unitarians in Boston (who frowned on Emerson's heresies), commented:

So, then, these rank "Leaves" have sprouted afresh, and in greater abundance. We hoped that they had dropped, and we should hear no more of them. But since they thrust themselves upon us again, with the pertinacity that is proverbial of noxious weeds . . . we can no longer refrain from speaking of them as we think they deserve. For here is not a question of literary opinion principally, but of the very essence of religion and morality. . . . We are bound in conscience to call it impious and obscene. . . . It sets off upon a sort of distracted philosophy, and openly deifies the bodily organs, senses, and appetites, in terms that admit of no double sense. To its pantheism and libidinousness it adds the most ridiculous swell of self-applause; for the author is "one of the roughs, a kosmos, disorderly, fleshy, sensual, divine inside and out."[9]

But *The Christian Spiritualist*, a Swedenborgian magazine, saw Whitman's poems as a transition from "the diseased mentalities of the past" to a new and purer "Spirit-life." This new poet was in "heart-sympathy with man, as he now is, struggling to free himself from the tyranny of the old and effete, and to grasp and retain the new life flowing down from heaven":

Such we conceive to be the interior condition of the author of "Leaves of Grass." He accepts man as he is as to his whole nature, and all men as his own brothers. The lambent flame of his genius encircles the world . . . There is a wild strength, a Spartan simplicity about the man, and he stalks among the dapper gentlemen of this generation, like a drunken Hercules amid the dainty dancers. . . . the book abounds in passages that cannot be quoted in drawing-rooms, and expressions that fall upon the tympanum of ears polite, with a terrible dissonance. His very gait, as he walks through the world, makes dainty People nervous; and conservatives regard him as a social revolution. His style is everywhere graphic and strong, and he sings things before untouched in prose or rhyme, in an idiom that is neither prose nor rhyme, nor yet orthodox blank verse. But it serves his purpose well. He wears his strange garb, cut and made by himself, as gracefully as a South American cavalier his poncho.[10]

That in 1856 Whitman's poems could both repel and attract an intelligent reader was most interestingly revealed by the reviewer of the second edition in *The New York Times*.[11] He professed sympathy with the poet's desire to turn his back on all shams and pretenses, to "fling off all moral clothing and walk naked over the earth," but he feared "the time is not yet come for the nakedness of purity," and that men are "not yet virtuous enough" to read Whitman's poems aloud to their children and wives. "What might be pastoral simplicity five hundred years hence, would perhaps be stigmatized as the coarsest indecency now—we regret to think that you [Mr. Whitman] have spoken too soon." Though vigorously condemning Whitman's "Phallic worship," and warning the poet that "the many indecencies" in his book would prevent it from finding "its way into many families," this critic confessed that he was fascinated by it:

> With all this muck of abomination soiling the paper, there is a wondrous, unaccountable fascination about the *Leaves of Grass*. As we read it again and again, and will confess that we have turned to it often, a singular order seems to arise out of its chaotic verses. Out of the mire and slough edged thoughts and keen philosophy starts suddenly, as the men of Cadmus sprang from the muddy loam. A lofty purpose still dominates the uncleanness and the ridiculous self-conceit in which the author, led astray by ignorance indulges.[12]

2

Aside from revealing what aspects of Whitman's poems most affronted the literary and moral sensibilities of mid-nineteenth-century Americans, these critics were also responsible for fostering several myths about the poet and his book, some of which have persisted down to the present time. One myth was that his shocking eccentricities were the result of ignorance; he was like a self-taught fireman or bus driver who had read and partly understood Emerson. He offended good taste because he did not know what good taste was. Many educated readers assumed that his strange verse-form, his bold language, and his daring metaphors could not have been created by anyone who knew established standards. Critics also thought that Whitman wrote unashamedly of sex because he was depraved—a second myth. Even the *Times* critic, who credited the poet with intentionally exposing moral sham and pretense, said Whitman was guilty of poor judgment which would doom his book to failure.

Whitman had, indeed, received little formal education, but he had read widely before writing his 1855 edition. He was the son of an unsuccessful and embittered carpenter and had grown up in the slums of Brooklyn, but in printing offices and later as editor of several newspapers, including the important Brooklyn *Eagle*, he had acquired considerable knowledge both of the world and of books. Though in his leisure hours he preferred to associate with firemen, omnibus drivers, and pilots of boats and ferries (Norton may have heard of his social habits), he was also avidly fond of the theater and Italian opera. Both in mind and in character he was an extremely complicated man. His sexual psychology was also puzzling, and biographers later discovered that he was homosexually inclined, psychologically if not in practice—on this point there has been wide disagreement.[13] But though contemptuous of organized churches and creeds, Whitman was deeply religious, and he always regarded religious motifs in his poems as their leading characteristics.

A third myth Whitman was primarily responsible for creating and perpetuating himself, and this is also a complicated subject. In the summer of 1855, when reviews of his book had scarcely had time to appear, Whitman began secretly writing his own reviews. This practice has also been attributed to his ignorance, but the ex-editor and journalist of wide experience knew the game of publicity only too well. Yet at the same time one must admit he believed so strongly in his message, regarding it as so urgently needed by his country, that he was unwilling to trust to chance for its reception. Convinced that America had not yet achieved a literature of real value, he taunted the established authors in his 1855 Preface, and probably expected them either to ignore or to denounce him. Like Norman Mailer a century later, he resorted to advertising himself.

Literary nationalism had been growing more strident each decade since the War of 1812, when Americans began to have confidence in their own strength. In his essay "The Poet" Emerson had declared that ". . . America is a poem in our eyes; its ample geography dazzles the imagination, and it will not wait long for meters." Whitman no doubt thought he was fulfilling Emerson's prophecy. He had written his rhapsodic 1855 Preface to call attention to his role as the spokesman of American democracy. In the 1855 poems themselves, nationalism is not especially conspicuous, if at all, and recent critics have been impressed by the mystic, or simply the lyricist, who wrote these poems, rather than "the poet of Democracy." Malcolm Cowley thinks that Whitman wrote his Preface for propaganda after he had composed the poems under different impulses and more genuine experiences.[14] But Whitman was not content to let his poems speak for themselves, or even his Preface. During the summer of 1855 he wrote three reviews,[15] which were promptly published in the *United States Review* (formerly the *Democratic Review*), the Brooklyn *Times*, and the *Phrenological Journal*. The review in the first of these began:

> An American bard at last! One of the roughs, large, proud, affectionate, eating, drinking, and breeding, his costume manly and free, his face sunburnt and bearded, his posture strong and erect, his voice bringing hope and prophecy to the generous races of young and old. We shall cease shamming and be what we

really are. We shall start an athletic and defiant literature. We realize how it is, and what was most lacking. . . . One sees unmistakably genteel persons, travelled, college-learned, used to be served by servants, conversing without heat or vulgarity, supported on chairs, or walking through handsomely carpeted parlors, or along shelves bearing well-bound volumes . . . and china things, and nicknacks. But where in American literature is the first show of America? Where are the gristle and beards, and broad breasts, and space and ruggedness, and nonchalance, that the souls of the people love?[16]

The Brooklyn *Times* review stated: "To give judgment on real poems, one needs an account of the poet himself." But the account merely gave more descriptions of the same "naïve, masculine, affectionate, contemplative, sensual, imperious person . . . ignorant or silently scornful, as at first appears, of all except his own presence and experience . . . Politeness this man has none, and regulation he has none. A rude child of the people!—No imitation—No foreigner—but a growth and idiom of America." This contains suggestions of the other three myths mentioned above, plus a little more jingoism and some echoes of the contemporary Native American or Know-Nothing political party, with its paranoiac suspicion of foreigners. This "rude child of the people," a combination of Paul Bunyan and the "Bowery Bhoy,"[17] the American superman-poet, is myth number four, appealingly symbolical and deceptively exaggerated.

A myth, like a caricature, is based on reality which is intentionally distorted to gain emphasis or emotional appeal. All these myths about Whitman and his poems contain some truth, and, intelligently interpreted, they yield insight into the poet and his work. But, if taken too seriously, they may also obscure the work, or become a cheap substitute for it, as a century of biography and criticism have demonstrated time and again.

One more comment on these myths is needed. In flaunting his rudeness and scorn of all refinements, Whitman aroused the class-conscious fears of such genteel critics and literary historians as Barrett Wendell, professor of English at Harvard College and personal friend of the "Boston Brahmins." In his *Literary History of America* published in 1901 he could not ignore Whitman, and he gave him equal space with Longfellow and Whittier. But his sympathies were with Lowell, who "lived all his life amid the gentlest academic and social influences of America," and Whittier, who, though of humble origin, "lived almost all of his life amid guileless influences."[18] But Walt Whitman, "born of the artisan class in a region close to the most considerable and corrupt centre of population on his native continent," held a "conception of equality utterly ignoring values," which Wendell saw as a danger to the American nation. Wendell knew that society was changing, but the increasing political power of the recent immigrants crowding the "New York slums and dingy suburban country" portended a future he could only anticipate with horror: "Those of us who love the past are far from sharing his [Whitman's] confidence in the future."[19] But Barrett Wendell was an honest man, and he had to confess that the "substance of Whitman's poems,—their imagery as distinguished from their form, or their spirit—comes wholly from our native country. . . . He can make you feel for the moment how even the ferry-boats plying from New York to Brooklyn are fragments of God's eternities."[20]

II THE FOREGROUND

I greet you at the beginning of a great career, which yet must
have had a long foreground somewhere, for such a start.
                                    —R. W. Emerson to Walt Whitman

1

The "long foreground" which Emerson, in complete ignorance
of Whitman's life, suspected "for such a start" as the first
Leaves of Grass has been a subject of speculation among scholars and critics ever since 1855.[1] The poems which *Walter*
Whitman contributed during the 1840s to popular magazines
were so conventional, sentimental, and trite that it seems
almost a miracle that *Walt* Whitman could have written the
1855 poems. Many critics have, in fact, declared that it was a
miracle,[2] though they usually called it the result of a "mystical
experience"—which, if genuine, is a kind of miracle. Although
mysticism seems to defy the laws of nature and is still a puzzle
to rational minds, the psychological characteristics of a "mystical experience" have been objectively described by William
James in *Varieties of Religious Experience*.[3] But Whitman
himself in all his reminiscences never mentioned having had

anything resembling the kind of experience James calls "mystical," which may be described briefly as the conviction that a Divine (or Cosmic) Consciousness[4] had on a certain occasion (sometimes repeatedly) flowed into a person's finite consciousness, leaving after-effects which in some cases have lasted for the remainder of the person's life. The only "evidence" any critic or biographer has ever found is Whitman's description of the mating of his body and soul, in a kind of sexual embrace, in section 5 of "Song of Myself." Interpretations of this passage will be discussed in Chapter IV, where the "mystical" approach to the *Leaves* will be evaluated.

Even though Whitman's earlier writing gave no promise of the great poems in *Leaves of Grass*, there was, nevertheless, a "foreground" of preparation, some knowledge of which may be helpful in understanding the nature and meaning of the *Leaves*. Even in the home of Whitman's uneducated parents there were attitudes and sympathies which gave direction to the development of the poet. First of all, both parents respected religion, though they were not members of any church and the only sermons they listened to were those of their friend Elias Hicks, a schismatic Quaker.[5] His heresy consisted in his doctrine that no restrictions whatever should be placed on an individual's religious convictions. All Quakers believed in an intuitive "inner light," but Hicks expanded this doctrine to the widest religious freedom. He denounced the doctrine that the chief end of man is "to glorify God, and seek and enjoy Him forever." Man's only duty here on earth, Hicks preached, is to enjoy life to the fullest extent, guided only by the "Deity-planted" intuitions of one's own soul.

This Hicksite doctrine, which closely resembled Emerson's later "Self Reliance," became the very foundation of Walt Whitman's own private religion, and he would always have a tender feeling for Quaker customs, such as the Quaker's proud refusal to doff his hat to man or God and his devotion to plain dress and plain speech. Whitman's maternal grandmother, Naomi Williams Van Velsor, was remembered by her grandson as "my grandmother Amy's sweet old face in its Quaker cap ..."[6] The Quakers were at least partly responsible for Whitman's belief that all physical life is dependent upon and sustained by an infinite spiritual realm about which a human being may have intuitive knowledge. It is not surprising that he later found Emerson a great stimulation to his development as a poet, for Whitman was a "transcendentalist" by conviction before he had ever heard of New England Transcendentalism.

In his youth Whitman had, apparently, little affection for his father. Yet his father in his own blind way also contributed to the "radical" political and social attitudes of his son who would become a poet. Walter Senior was a great admirer of the notorious socialist Frances ("Fanny") Wright, and Walt remembered having accompanied his father to her lectures in Brooklyn and New York City.[7] In old age he could say of this "most maligned, lied-about" woman, "She has always been to me one of the sweetest of sweet memories. . . . I never felt so glowingly toward any other woman."[8]

Walt Whitman never became a socialist, but his sympathy for the working man, his suspicion of wealth, and his contempt for "polite society" were acquired from his father and such heroes and heroines of his father as Fanny Wright. These early-acquired attitudes also influenced him to champion the "free soil" movement, and to work for the Free Soil Party in 1848 when Martin Van Buren ran for the Presidency and Charles Francis Adams for the Vice-Presidency. This was the cause of Whitman's losing the editorship of the Brooklyn *Eagle*, which was controlled by the "Old Hunkers," the conservative old-line

Democrats who dominated the party in New York State. Although Whitman never actively worked for abolition, he did write articles and editorials on the inhumanity of slavery, and the second poem in date of composition to be included in *Leaves of Grass* is "A Boston Ballad," a bitter satire on the Boston authorities who arrested the runaway slave Anthony Burns and returned him to his Virginia owner in June 1854.[9]

The poet of "Song of Myself" suffered vicariously the torments of the "hounded slave" (829–39), and in fantasy brought help to the sick and oppressed everywhere. His compassionate temperament Whitman probably inherited from his Dutch mother, but his politics and identification with all unfortunate people were taught him by his fiercely egalitarian father.

One of Walter Senior's personal friends was Tom Paine, who lived in Brooklyn, neglected and even hated by the nation he had helped to win its independence from Britain. Paine's *Age of Reason*—Deistic, not atheistic, as the priests claimed—was one of the Whitman family's most prized books. Walt's lifelong anticlericalism was no doubt derived partly from this book, as well as from his own father, but there were other sources for it too. One of these was Count Volney's *Ruins; or Meditations on the Revolutions of Empires*,[10] which regarded the priest as one of the tyrants who had enslaved mankind. Volney was a *philosophe* who contributed to the French Revolution. But what Whitman got from his book, which he had read at home, was less the Existentialism of Volney (man's destiny "is not concealed in the bosom of the divinity; it resides in man himself . . .") than an interest in the history of the human race and the religions of different nations, which Volney surveyed. Whitman learned to respect all religions, without accepting any one, and as a poet he seriously cherished the idea of extracting the best of every religion to form a new eclectic religion to be introduced in his poems. In this new religion for a truly democratic society (more of a philosophy than a sect), man would worship the divinity incarnated in himself.

Another book which Whitman read in his youth was Fanny Wright's *A Few Days in Athens*.[11] He read this book so attentively that he later many times echoed, paraphrased, and perhaps unconsciously quoted it in his poems. Miss Wright attempted to popularize the philosophy of Epicurus by a fictional account of debates between the disciples of Epicurean and of Stoic philosophy, with a final oration by Epicurus himself. Again, only part of the doctrine could have appealed to young Whitman, for Epicurus, like Lucretius, taught that religion is "the bane of human happiness, perverter of human virtue. . . . [The] source of every enjoyment is within yourself. Good and evil lie before you. The good is—all which can yield pleasure: the evil—what must bring pain." Religion denies this doctrine. The so-called lower animals "exercise the faculties they possess . . . Man alone . . . doubts the evidence of his superior senses . . . and turns to poison all the sources of his happiness." This teaching evidently appealed to the poet who longed in "Song of Myself" to "turn and live with the animals . . . so placid and self-contained" (sec. 32).

Yet in spite of Epicurus's blaming man's unhappiness on religion, *A Few Days in Athens* contained suggestions of a Lucretian naturalistic religion—perhaps causing Whitman later to read *De Rerum Natura* and outline it book by book.[12] In *A Few Days*, Metrodorous declares that "everything is eternal," composed of unchangeable atoms that produce all the varieties in the substances constituting "the great material whole, of which we form a part." The atoms may form part of a vegetable today, and an animal tomorrow, which in perishing forms other vegetables and animals. This is the same doctrine the poet of "Song of Myself" voices near the end of the poem: "I bequeath myself to the dirt to grow from the grass I love, / If you want me again look for me under your bootsoles." But Whitman's joyous acceptance of death as part of the natural cycle of life and rebirth was more like Lucretius's attempt through his poem to abolish the fear of death; death is good because it is natural. In the same spirit Whitman would call the grass in "Song of Myself" "the beautiful uncut hair of graves" (101) and declare that "the smallest sprout shows there is really no death" (117).

A *Few Days in Athens* may have given Whitman only a few hints, or, more likely, confirmed some of his own intellectual predilections, but some of the parallels between this book and Whitman's ideas in his poems are striking enough to clarify certain themes and motifs in the poems. For example: ". . . all existences are equally wonderful. An African lion is in himself nothing more extraordinary than a Grecian horse; although the whole people of Athens will assemble to gaze on the lion, and exclaim, 'How wonderful!' while no man observes the horse."[13] One of the major themes in "Song of Myself" is that every thing that exists is equally wonderful: "And there is no object so soft but it makes a hub for the wheeled universe. . . ." (1269). And underlying this equality of matter, "all theology with fear and duty in its creed should be banished," for "It is love—love alone that can be claimed by Gods or yielded by man."

2

Every influence in his home, his reading, and the demands of his insatiable psyche instilled in the youthful Walter Whitman a revulsion against theologies based on fear and duty and impelled him toward a religion whose only creed was love. This is plainly evident in his memory of the Bible. He must have read the Bible with remarkable attention to have been able to allude to it and quote from it so extensively in his writings, especially in his juvenile poetry and prose preceding *Leaves of Grass*. But it was the New Testament and the God of love which made the deeper impression upon him, to judge by the frequency of his allusions to the life and death of Christ rather than to the persons and events of the Old Testament.[14]

One critic has surmised that the role of the poet as healer and consoler in "Song of Myself" was foreshadowed in the juvenile short story "Shirval,"[15] based on the account of Christ's restoring life to the son of the widow of Nain (Luke 7:11–16). Indeed, the creed Whitman enunciated in his 1855 Preface to *Leaves of Grass* is almost straight out of the New Testament, though modified by Paine's Deism and Elias Hicks's radical Quakerism:

This is what you shall do: Love the earth and sun and the animals, despise riches, give alms to every one that asks, stand up for the stupid and crazy, devote your income and labor to others, hate tyrants, argue not concerning God, have patience and indulgence toward the people, take off your hat to nothing known or unknown or to any man or number of men, go freely with powerful uneducated persons and with the young and with the mothers of families, read these leaves in the open air every season of every year of your life, re-examine all you have been told at school or church or in any book, dismiss whatever insults your own soul, and your very flesh shall be a great poem and have the richest fluency not only in words but in the silent lines of its lips and face and between the lashes of your eyes and in every motion and joint of your body.[16]

In this same Preface we find: "There will soon be no more priests, their work is done." But the "superior breed . . . of priests of man," Whitman prophesies, will take their place, by which he means the kind of poet he is striving to become. Eventually in *Passage to India* he will call the poet "the true son of God." The poet who attempted to play this lofty role in *Leaves of Grass* never ceased to draw inspiration from the Hebraic and Christian Scriptures which he so thoroughly absorbed in his youth. What the Old Testament meant to him is indicated in *Democratic Vistas*: "Hebrew prophet, with spirituality, as in flashes of lightning, conscience like red-hot iron, plaintive songs and screams of vengeance for tyrannies and enslavement; Christ with bent head, brooding love and peace, like a dove."[17] No book is more conspicuous in Walt Whitman's "long foreground" than the King James Bible.

Whitman compensated for his lack of formal education by reading so voraciously during his youth and early manhood that it would be tedious to survey all the books and authors he read, and unprofitable because many of them throw only feeble or indirect light on his mature writings, though some probably influenced his intellectual development in deep and subtle ways. In his youth, for example, he devoured the romances of Sir Walter Scott and the sketches and novels of Dickens.[18] His journalistic writings before 1850 often reflected his interest in Scott and Dickens, especially the latter, but *Leaves of Grass* scarcely at all. Whitman read Homer, in at least two translations; also the Greek dramas, Shakespeare, Dante, Milton, and of course the Romantic poets of Great Britain.[19] A great favorite, George Sand,[20] may have given him some hints of the kind of wandering poet he dreamed of becoming, but this ambition was fed by so many springs, personal, cultural, and literary, that it seems almost hopeless to search for the "true" source, and all attempts by scholars and critics have failed. Certainly at one period Emerson's "American Scholar" was one of Whitman's "springs of courage,"[21] as one critic has called it. The 1855 Preface to *Leaves of Grass* has sometimes been regarded as hardly more than Whitman's variations on Emerson's theme.

Yet even the ideas of "The American Scholar" could and did reach Whitman from many directions, for in 1837 Emerson's contribution was mainly to put into eloquent language the ideas and convictions of the majority of literary minds in the United States in the third decade of the nineteenth century. The doctrine of nationalism in art and literature was not confined to America, for it was a basic tenet of the Romantic movement, from Lessing and the Schlegels in Germany to Madame de Staël in France, to Wordsworth in England, and their numerous progeny in many countries. But the upsurge of American pride after the defeat of Great Britain in the War of 1812 naturally gave a great impetus to literary nationalism in the United States. As a journalist during the 1840 decade, when this nationalism was reaching a frenzy of intensity, Walt Whitman was bombarded from all sides by appeals for an indigenous and democratic literature, purified of the aristocratic poisons of feudalistic Europe. Although Shakespeare was Whitman's favorite author, he would never be able to enjoy him without a guilty conscience,[22] because he wrote in an aristocratic age.

In the second issue of his 1855 *Leaves of Grass* Whitman printed a selection from reviews of the book, but at the top of these he quoted three long paragraphs from Edwin T. Whipple's 1844 review of Rufus Griswold's *Poets and Poetry of America*. The prominence of this extract makes it almost a "text" for the reprinted reviews of Whitman's book. In fact, one might suppose that he proposed it as an "epigraph" (to use T. S. Eliot's term) for *Leaves of Grass*, as perhaps it had been for the poet in writing the poems. The three paragraphs are too long to quote entire, but here is the substance:

We can hardly conceive, that a reasonable being should look with coldness or dislike upon any efforts to establish a national literature, of which poetry is such an important element. . . . The life of our native land,—the inner spirit which animates its institutions,—the new ideas and principles of which it is the representative,—these every patriot must wish to behold reflected from the broad mirror of a comprehensive and soul-animating literature. The true vitality of a nation is not seen in the triumphs of its industry, the extent of its conquests, or the reach of its empire; but in its intellectual dominion. Posterity passes over statistical tables of trade and population, to search for records of mind and heart. It is of little moment how many millions of men were included at any time under the name of one people, if they have left no intellectual testimonials of their mode and manner of existence. . . . A nation lives only through its literature, and its mental life is immortal. . . .

America abounds in the materials of poetry. Its history, its scenery, the structure of its social life, the thoughts which pervade its political forms, the meaning which underlies its hot contests, are all capable of being exhibited in a poetical aspect. Carlyle, in speaking of the settlement of Plymouth by the Pilgrims, remarked that, if we had the open sense of the Greeks, we should have "found a poem here; one of nature's own poems, such as she writes in broad facts over great continents." If we have a literature, it should be a national literature; no feeble or sonorous echo of Germany or England, but essentially American in its tone and object.

In order that America may take its due rank in the commonwealth of nations, a literature is needed which shall be the exponent of its higher life. . . . Beneath all the shrewdness and selfishness of the American character, there is a smouldering enthu-

siasm which flames out at the first touch of fire,—sometimes at
the hot and hasty words of party, and sometimes at the bidding
of great thoughts and unselfish principles. The heart of the
nation is easily stirred to its depths; but those who rouse its fiery
impulses into action are often men compounded of ignorance
and wickedness, and wholly unfit to guide the passions which
they are able to excite. There is no country in the world which
has nobler ideas embodied in more worthless shapes. All our fac-
tions, fanaticisms, reforms, parties, creeds, ridiculous or danger-
ous though they often appear, are founded on some aspiration or
reality which deserves a better form and expression. . . . We want
a poetry which shall speak in clear, loud tones to the people; a
poetry which shall make us more in love with our native land, by
converting its ennobling scenery into the images of lofty
thoughts; . . . give new power to the voice of conscience, and
new vitality to human affection; soften and elevate passion:
guide enthusiasm in a right direction; and speak out in the high
language of men to a nation of men.[23]

Except for the "organic principle" (*i.e.*, poems should grow
naturally, like lilacs on a bush or melons on the vine), the substance of Whitman's concept of the nature and functions of
the American poet is almost all here in Whipple's plea for a
national literature. But Whipple's expression is formal and
abstract. Whitman's genius gave the ideas a more imaginative
expression, and converted the nationalistic concepts, already
hackneyed from decades of repetition, into the language of
poetry.

3

One other suspected or possible source of Whitman's "long
foreground" has never been satisfactorily investigated, and
remains as elusive as his "mystical experience." In fact, it is the

mysticism that many readers have thought they found in certain of Whitman's poems which encourages this search for its fountainhead in the ancient literature of India—and to some extent in other Oriental writings. Emerson may have suspected some knowledge of the old Hindu poems somewhere in the "long foreground," for he himself was deeply interested in the literature of India—and would have detected the striking parallels that other readers soon began to point out.

When Thoreau visited Whitman in 1856, he told the poet that he found *Leaves of Grass* "wonderfully like the Orientals . . . ," and asked if Whitman had read them (meaning, apparently, the Sanscrit poems), but the answer was: "No: Tell me about them."[24] Whether this answer was deceptive, modest, or candid remains debatable. Many years later Whitman named, along with the great works in world literature, "the ancient Hindoo poems" as "embryonic facts of 'Leaves of Grass.' "[25] The reference is so ambiguous that one scarcely knows how seriously to take it. Most of the early commentators on the Oriental echoes or parallels in the *Leaves* assumed that Whitman had derived the similarities by indirect influences rather than the actual reading of translations. In 1866 Lord Strangford, a distinguished British Orientalist, thought Whitman's verse technique pure Persian, imbued "with not only the spirit, but with the veriest mannerism, and most absolute trick and accent of Persian poetry . . ."[26]

Two decades later, the French scholar Gabriel Sarrazin wrote: "Walt Whitman, in his confident and lofty piety, is the direct inheritor of the great Oriental mystics, Brahma, Proclus, Abou Saïd."[27] Edward Carpenter, a British poet who imitated Whitman and visited him in 1877, declared in 1906: "In the Vedic scriptures, and, in lineal succession from these, in the Buddhist and Platonist and Christian writings, in the Taoist of China, the Mystics of Egypt, the Sufis of Persia, the root is to be found—and is clearly distinguishable—the very same from which 'Leaves of Grass' has sprung."[28]

Carpenter even compiled a list of parallel passages in *Leaves of Grass* and the Upanishads, *Mahâparinibbâna Suttanta*, *Bhagavad Gita*, and *Sayings of Lao-tzu*. But he claimed for these parallels no more than that "all down history the same loving universal spirit has looked out, making its voice heard from time to time, harmonizing the diverse eras, enclosing continents, castes, and theologies."[29] More specifically, an Indian is quoted by William Guthrie as saying that Whitman "must have studied *The Bhagavad Gita*, for in *Leaves of Grass* one finds the teachings of Vedanta; the Song of Myself is but an echo of the sayings of Krishna."[30]

The first scholar to examine in detail the Vedanta parallels was Dorothy Frederica Mercer, who completed a doctoral dissertation in 1933 at the University of California on "Leaves of Grass and the Bhagavad Gita: A Comparative Study."[31] She found a basic similarity in the doctrine of the *self*: "Whitman's soul, like the self of the *Bhagavad Gita*, is the unifying energy . . . it is Brahma incarnated in the body; and it is permanent, indestructible, all-pervading, unmanifest." ("Soul" is here used in the sense of the symbolical "I" in "Song of Myself" and other poems.) Dr. Mercer's study was followed by a more systematic investigaton at Benares Hindu University in India by V. K. Chari, who in 1956 completed a dissertation on "Whitman and Indian Thought: an Interpretation in the Light of Vedantic Mysticism"—published in the United States in 1964 as *Whitman in the Light of Vedantic Mysticism*. Dr. Chari found that "The subject matter of Whitman's poetry is no other than the nature of experience itself, an intimate and vital concern with and a close attention to the fact of human consciousness."[32] Chari was not interested in whether Whitman had known the Upanishads or not, but in interpreting *Leaves of Grass* in terms of the ancient Indian logic developed by such teachers as Sankara.

These examples of writers who have suggested Oriental works either as sources or as significant parallels for Whitman's poems have been mentioned to show that his "long foreground" has cast a very long shadow, possibly reaching even from India to Long Island. Whether Whitman did read the "ancient Hindoo poems" in translation, or whether the passages proposed as parallels actually are close enough to be significant, is not as important as the fact that repeatedly intelligent readers have been reminded of various Oriental works as they read Whitman.[33]

4

Not all of Whitman's "long foreground" was useful to him—or at least its use conflicted with other purposes and literary motifs which he strove to express in his poems. One of these influences was the "Young America" literary movement of the 1840 decade led by John L. O'Sullivan, editor of the *Democratic Review*, and a group of literary critics who shared his views.[34] During this decade the *Democratic Review* was friendly to Walter Whitman and published a number of his "popular" short stories and poems. Even later, after he had metamorphosed into an almost totally different kind of poet, Whitman still remembered the magazine with gratitude and approval. In 1858, nine years after the decease of the *Democratic Review*, Whitman called it "a monthly magazine of a profounder quality of talent than any since," especially important to "the young men" of the early 1840s.

The beginning of the Young America movement seemed little more than another demand for a national literature, and O'Sullivan is remembered as the coiner of the phrase "manifest destiny" to justify the expansion of the United States to the Pacific Ocean. But the critics who joined the Young America movement were interested in more than expansion and the growth of an empire, or in achieving literary independence from Great Britain. They wanted to use literature to help create a more democratic society—an ideal not unlike that of the Russians a century later in using Social Realism to build a Communist society.

The Young Americans were all Jacksonian Democrats, or Locofocos, as Walt Whitman was also at the time; and because they were strongly partisan, they were savagely attacked by the Whigs as subversive to religion, 'morality, and good manners. Like all the other nationalists, the Young Americans looked for a poet who would achieve a place in world literature as the American Homer.[35] They scorned contemporary American authors not only for being imitative of European authors but especially for not having emanicapted themselves from their aristocratic heritage. They called for a "literature for the people," a "poetry for the mass," by which they meant that their ideal poet not only must be able to exalt the dignity of labor and the honor of poverty, "the brotherhood and equality of all men," the evil consequence of "distinctions of rank and wealth," but also must be able to speak directly to the common people, bolster their courage in the continual struggle against privilege, and foster a truly *democratic* society. Among the British poets they praised were Burns, Crabbe, and Wordsworth —poets who had sprung from the people and spoke their language. Emerson they first praised and then criticized for being too aloof from the life and needs of the masses.[36]

This theory led the Young America critics to focus attention on the poet, the creator of the poem, rather than his creation. How could he understand the people and speak to them unless he himself was of humble origin and had lived with common people? Perhaps this part of the Young America theory appealed to Walt Whitman because he was the son of a carpenter and had grown up in an artisan community. Actually, Whitman nowhere in his published writings referred to the Young Americans and he took no part at the time in their campaign, possibly because he was too busy writing his conventional stories and poems—which did, however, appeal to the literary taste of the masses at that time. In this sense he did "speak to the people," but not the social message which these critics were advocating; yet not because he did not agree with them, for in his editorials in the Brooklyn *Eagle* (1846–48) he shared most of their social attitudes and patriotic ambitions.[37]

After the *Democratic Review* expired in 1849, the clamor of the Young America critics subsided. It is entirely possible that Whitman never realized that he owed any debt to them. But, as we have seen, in his self-written reviews of the first *Leaves of Grass* he advertised himself as "An American bard at last! One of the roughs. . . . A rude child of the people!"[38] And almost the whole of his 1855 Preface was either an adaptation or an expansion of the Young America theory, as in his declaration that "The largeness of nature or the nation were monstrous without a corresponding largeness and generosity of the spirit of the citizen." This would become Whitman's central theory of the function of literature: to aid the growth of moral character. "An individual is as superb as a nation when he has the qualities which make a superb nation."[39] Whitman never deviated from his ambition to exhibit in his poems the archetype-self needed for an ideal democratic society. Of course, to attain this health-giving influence on the masses he must be read by them, and in 1855 he felt so sure of success in this ambition that he closed his Preface with these words: "The proof of a poet is

that his country absorbs him as affectionately as he has
absorbed it."

Of all Walt Whitman's failures, his bitterest was his inabil-
ity to meet his own test of his worth as a poet. In the course of
time he came to be praised by friendly critics and biographers
as the "poet of democracy," but he would never be read by the
masses. His own mother and his brothers and sisters did not
understand his poems.[40] Nor did few if any of the omnibus
drivers, ferryboat pilots, or wounded soldiers in Civil War hospitals, the men whose companionship gave him most pleasure
and satisfaction. That he was indeed a poet, even a great one,
was first recognized by educated men and women, especially
poets, critics, artists—intellectuals. This is the great contradiction between Whitman's literary theory and his actual achievement as a poet.

5

The contradiction between Whitman's theory (and ambition) and his actual achievement in his poems existed even in
the preparatory stages of *Leaves of Grass*, as his notebooks
clearly reveal. In the first place, from the very beginning in his
new role as "a poet of the people" he was not concerned with
average, living Americans but with an ideal archetype:

> True noble expanded American Character is raised on a far
> more lasting and universal basis than that of any of the characters
> of the "gentlemen" of aristocratic life, or of novels, or under the
> European or Asian forms of society or government.—It is to be
> illimitably proud, independent, self-possessed, generous and
> gentle. It is to accept nothing except what is equally free and eli-
> gible to any body else. It is to be poor, rather than rich—but to

prefer death sooner than any mean dependence.—Prudence is
part of it, because prudence is the right arm of independence.[41]

No doubt, average Americans also thought of themselves not
as they were but as they hoped to be, and Whitman in this 1847
notation epitomized their dream. But few could have had the
sophistication to see how far such a dream transcended the
actuality. That Whitman did is evidenced by a later notebook
passage (probably written a year later):

> Our country seems to be threatened with a sort of ossification
> of the spirit. Amid all the advanced grandeurs of these times
> beyond any other of which we know—amid the never enough
> praised spread of common education and common newspapers
> and books—amid the universal accessibility of riches and per-
> sonal comforts—the wonderful inventions—the cheap swift
> travel bringing far nations together—amid all the extreme
> reforms and benevolent societies—the current that bears us is
> one broadly and deeply materialistic and infidel. It is the very
> worst of infidelity because it suspects not itself but proceeds com-
> placently onward and abounds in churches and all the days of its
> life solves never the simple riddle why it has not a good
> time.—For I do not believe the people of these days are happy.
> The public countenance lacks its bloom of love and its freshness
> of faith.—For want of these, it is cadaverous as a corpse.[42]

The point emphasized here is that Whitman the former journalist knew his contemporary society in realistic detail, but in
planning to assume the role of poet of his nation he became a
complete idealist, with the consequence that the America of his
poems is a dream-world, though he fervently hoped to turn the
dream into reality. But he approached this transformation not
through social or political programs but through metaphysics,
derived in part from the Transcendentalism of Carlyle and

Emerson. A major theme in Whitman's poems, the Lucretian idea that the body and the soul are one, would be reached only after much notebook pondering on the nature of the soul and its relation to the material world. Thus, in the 1847 notebook:

The soul or spirit transmits itself into all matter—into rocks, and can live the life of a rock—into the sea, and can feel itself the sea—into the oak, or other tree—into an animal, and feel itself a horse, a fish, or bird—into the earth—into the motions of the sun and stars—

Then, more clearly Neo-Platonic:

The effusion or corporation of the soul is always under the beautiful laws of physiology—I guess the soul itself can never be anything but great and pure and immortal; but it makes itself visible only through matter—a perfect head, and bowels and bones to match is the easy gate through which it comes from its embowered garden, and pleasantly appears to the sight of the world.—A twisted skull, and blood watery or rotten by ancestry or gluttony, or rum or bad disorders,—they are the darkness toward which the plant will not grow, although its seed lies waiting for ages.—[43]

But Whitman goes beyond Neo-Platonism in his notebook doctrine of "dilation," which gives the poet's soul the power of growth without limit or material restriction:

I think the soul will never stop, or attain to any growth beyond which it shall not go.—When I walked at night by the sea shore and looked up at the countless stars, I asked of my soul whether it would be filled and satisfied when it should become god enfolding all these, and open to the life and delight and knowledge of everything in them or of them; and the answer was plain to me at the breaking water on the sands at my feet: the answer was, No, when I reach there, I shall want to go further still.—44

Yet "spirit is not greater than matter," for it abides in the material existence:

When I see where the east is greater than the west,—where the sound man's part of the child is greater than the sound woman's part—or where a father is more needful than a mother to produce me—then I guess I shall see how spirit is greater than matter.—Here the run of poets and the learned always strike, and here shoots the ballast of many a grand head.—My life is a miracle and my body which lives is a miracle; but of what I can nibble at the edges of the limitless and delicious wonder I know that I cannot separate them, and call one superior and the other inferior, any more than I can say my sight is greater than my eyes.—

You have been told that mind is greater than matter [unfinished]

I cannot understand the mystery, but I am always conscious of myself as two—as my soul [conscience?] and I: and I reckon it is the same with all men and women.—45

That "life is a miracle" will be the burden of this poet's message in his major poem "Song of Myself," and he will convey it as he makes his readers *see* by opening the windows, the "oval gates" (their eyes), to the beauties of the physical world:

I will not be a great philosopher, and found any school, and build it with iron pillars, and gather the young men around me, and make them my disciples, that new superior churches and politics shall come.—But I will take each man and woman of you to the window and open the shutters and the sash, and my left arm shall hook you round the waist, and my right shall point you to the endless and beginningless road along whose sides are crowded the rich cities of all living philosophy, and oval gates that pass you in to fields of clover and landscapes clumped with sassafras, and orchards of good apples, and every breath through your mouth shall be of a new perfumed and elastic air, which is love.—Not I—not God—can travel this road for you.—It is not far, it is within the stretch of your thumb; perhaps you shall find it every where over the ocean and over the land, when you once have the vision to behold it.—[46]

But to attain this "vision" of the external world, a man's inner vision must be in focus. If he eats his bread in the presence of starving men and does not divide with them, his soul will "hiss like an angry snake, and say to him, 'Fool will you stuff your greed and starve me?' "[47]

The ignorant man is demented with the madness of owning things—of having by warranty deeds [in] court clerk's records, the right to mortgage, sell, give away or raise money on certain possessions.—But the wisest soul knows that no object can really be owned by one man or woman any more than another.—The orthodox proprietor says This is mine, I earned or received or paid for it,—and by positive right of my own I will put a fence around it, and keep it exclusively to myself. . . . He cannot share his friend or his wife because of them he is no owner, except by their love, and if any one gets that away from him, it is best not to curse, but quickly call the offal cart to his door and let physical wife or friend go, the tail with the hide.—[48]

This doctrine could have come either from the New Testament or from the Hindu "scripture" poems. Whitman must have been familiar with Emerson's recent (1846) treatment of the delusion of ownership in "Hamatreya," but Thoreau's *Walden,* with its running satire on the tyranny of *being owned* by things, would not be published until 1854. Whatever the source of this wisdom concerning worldly goods, Whitman would soon begin to neglect his business affairs and start pre-

paring to live the role of his ideal poet, with its symbolical puri-
fication rites, sacrifices, and moral training. "Why can we not,"
he wrote in another notebook of this period, "see beings who
by the manliness and transparence of their natures, disarm the
entire world, and brings [sic] one and all to his side, as friends
and believers!"[49] Such a person Walt Whitman would be. But
the charisma he was now cultivating was not that of a Christian saint or an Oriental ascetic. Several sentences later in the
same paragraph quoted above he wrote:

> The first inspiration of real wisdom in our souls lets us know that
> the self will and wickedness and malignity we thought so
> unsightly in our race are by no means what we are told, but
> something far different, and not amiss except to spirits of the
> feeble and the shorn.—as the freckles and bristly beard of Jupiter
> to be removed by washes and razors, under the judgment of gen-
> teel squirts, but in the sight of the great master, proportionate
> and essential and sublime.—[50]

He would be a freckled, bearded Jupiter, not a St. Francis.
And Whitman's beard and informal dress would become symbols of his godlike pride in his independence. His confidence in
the development of his own soul and body rested in cosmic
"Amelioration . . . the blood that runs through the body of the
universe." In dramatizing what Amelioration seems to say, he
finds his own poetic voice:

> I do not lag—I do not hasten—I bide my hour over billions of
> billions of years—I exist in the void that takes uncounted time
> and coheres to a nebula, and in further time cohering to an orb,
> marches gladly round, a beautiful tangible creature, in his place
> in the procession of God, where new comers have been falling
> in[to] the ranks for ever, and will be so always—I could not be
> balked no how, not if all the worlds and living beings were this

minute reduced back into the impalpable film of chaos—I should surely bring up again where we now stand and go on as much further and thence on and on—My right hand is time, and my left hand is space—both are ample—a few quintillions of cycles, a few sextillions of cubic leagues, are not of importance to me—what I shall attain to I can never tell, for there is something that underlies me, of whom I am a part and instrument.[51]

Now he knows that "All truths lie waiting in all things," and that they will unfold to him "like roses from living buds" if he is prepared to receive the truth: "But it must be in yourself.—It shall come from your soul.—It shall be love." The ultimate truth, the leitmotif of his future poems, Whitman has found:

> We know that sympathy or love is the law over all laws, because in nothing else but love is the soul conscious of pure happiness, which appears to be the ultimate place, and point of all things.—[52]

6

T. S. Eliot said that mediocre poets borrow, genuine poets steal; by which he meant, evidently, that the real poet transforms what he borrows until he makes it his own. Whitman once declared: "Nature may have given the hint to the author of 'Leaves of Grass,' but there exists no book or fragment of a book which can have given the hint to them [sic]."[53] Perhaps he intended only to defend his originality, at a time when too many critics were asking about his debt to Emerson. But *no hint* is too strong a defense, for every author derives hints from many sources, some of which are half buried in his subconscious. However, sources for a literary work are important not because they indicate indebtedness but because they help the reader or critic to understand the kind of ideas or experiences which appealed to the author and found expression in his creations. They may, in short, remove some of the ambiguity of the language and clarify or intensify the meaning which a reader may encounter in it. Literary sources show as much about a poet's character and personality as his manner of composing his poems. Every author reads many books which he quickly forgets because they do not solve any personal problems for him, or they may have only given him confidence in ideas that he had before held with doubt or vagueness. The healthy mind retains what it needs. Sometimes a book can actually change the direction of one's life, but more often it merely strengthens one's intuition and predilections.

The psychoanalytic critic is usually more interested in the author's infantile relations with his parents than in the books he reads a few years later. Both are important, and the books the child reads may throw light on his relations with his parents—and the kind of parents they are. It is significant that in the Whitman home there were copies of *The Age of Reason*, *A Few Days in Athens*, and Volney's *Ruins*. And, equally important, that little Walter read these books, for there is no evidence that his brothers or sisters did—or if they did read them, the reading bore no visible results.

It is even, in fact, significant that Whitman was an avid reader in his youth. Since he was not ambitious for financial or professional success, he read because he was lonely, curious, or emotionally starved. The second child in a family of six boys and two girls, he may in childhood, as Edwin H. Miller argues, have felt neglected by his harassed mother.[54] By his own admission, he did not feel sympathy for his father until the last years of his father's life (he died in 1855). At the age of twelve the boy left his (probably uncongenial) home and began boarding with the printer to whom his father had apprenticed him. For many years thereafter he did not have a home of his own, and as Jean Catel has said,[55] the streets of Brooklyn and New York became his home. He found excitement in the crowds and the noise of the city traffic, yet in his teens when he went to the theater he liked to go alone because boys of his own age did not pay close attention to the voices on the stage. Even in a crowd, he lived much in his own thoughts.

Whitman's juvenile writings came, he said himself, from the surface of his mind.[56] He imitated the popular writers of the day and only partially represented himself in the melancholy of his "graveyard" poetry and his didactic stories of insensitive fathers, cruel schoolmasters, young men who succumbed to the temptations of the wicked city, and similar threadbare themes. He did not begin to discover his own literary ability until he began to tap the resources of his fantasy life: his concealed desire for heroic leadership, his need for a symbolical outlet for his dammed-up erotic impulses, the appeal of vicarious dreams of friendship—especially with young men—as a substitute for the intimate friend he could not find in reality, and above all else his yearning for the oceans of love which he felt himself so capable of sharing with someone, anyone, everyone. Many years later (1876), after he had suffered a stroke, partial paralysis, and many defeats in his literary ambitions, Whitman made a "full confession" which explains more frankly than any other confession he ever published the private source of his poems:

Something more may be added—for, while I am about it, I would make a full confession. I also sent out *Leaves of Grass* to arouse and set flowing in men's and women's hearts, young and old, (my present and future readers,) endless streams of living, pulsating love and friendship, directly from them to myself, now and ever. To this terrible, irrepressible yearning, (surely more or less down underneath in most human souls,) this never-satisfied appetite for sympathy, and this boundless offering of sympathy—this universal democratic comradeship—this old, eternal, yet ever-new interchange of adhesiveness, so fitly emblematic of America—I have given in this book, undisguisedly, declaredly, the openest expression.[57]

This "terrible, irrepressible yearning" was undoubtedly sexual in origin. It may have been stronger in Whitman than in some of his contemporaries, yet "surely more or less down underneath in most human souls." In his preparatory notebooks there is very little about sex, though the basis of the "sex program" in his poems could logically have developed from his Lucretian doctrine of the equality of mind and body, with special emphasis on the sacredness of the body and all its natural functions. But an abstract idea would not have suggested such words as *terrible, irrepressible, never-satisfied appetite* to describe his emotional needs for love and sympathy. One can hardly doubt that Whitman's passional urges caused him to embrace the idea that sex was a healthy, proper, and much-needed subject for a dynamic poetry. Throughout his lifetime many of his readers thought he defied society's rigid censorship of sex because he was depraved. Some early twentieth-century critics thought his defiance a sign of abnormality—and he was aberrant to the extent of exalting "adhesiveness" (a phrenological term[58] for affection between men) over "amativeness" (heterosexual attraction). But in his struggle to understand and come to terms with his own eroticism, abnormal or not, he found out the importance of sex in human experience and had the courage to express his knowledge in the face of enormous social pressure to conceal it.

What Whitman's discovery and his courage to express it meant to literature, Professor Edwin Miller has eloquently stated in his recent book, *Walt Whitman's Poetry: A Psychological Journey*:

> One of Whitman's most original contributions to our (and world) literature is his depiction of the narcissistic universe of the child and adolescent, not in the irrelevant terms of angelic youth with or without "intimations of immortality," but in terms of the dynamics of relationships (or their absence) and sexual maturation. When Whitman insists that the soul cannot be separated from the body he is alleging that man is fated to live by and with his body with all its insistent and frequently contradictory and anxiety-producing desires—as well as with its sensuous delights. . . . When he writes in "Song of Myself":

> > Divine am I inside and out, and I make holy whatever
> >   I touch or am touched from;
> > The scent of these arm-pits is aroma finer than prayer,
> > This head is more than churches or bibles or creeds.

he is protesting the human and emotional damage that results from a culturally imposed rejection of tactility and infantile sensuousness. Casting aside, more successfully than any other American writer of the century, the dark dress of American puritanism and Western inhibitions, he "undrapes" and dances like a Dionysian, or one of the "monsters" in Hawthorne's curiously ambivalent tale of "The Maypole of Merry Mount," to the very brink of Henry James's "abyss," and finds it good because it is human. . . . Whitman . . . rises above the half-truths that afflicted the brooding minds of his [literary] contemporaries: he perceives not only the "inferno" but also the "paradiso" granted to those not afraid of "the dazzle of the light and of every moment of your life."[59]

The "foreground" that Emerson suspected in Whitman's background could not have been this insight into human nature, because he, for all his greater knowledge of literature and philosophy, was one of the most inhibited poets of his period. Only Whitman could undrape and dance like a Dionysian.

III PERENNIAL LEAVES

Perennial roots, tall leaves, O the winter shall not freeze you
   delicate leaves,
Every year shall you bloom again . . .
                              —"Scented Herbage of My Breast"

1

The critic in the *Christian Examiner* (quoted in Chapter I) who regretted in 1856 that Whitman's "rank 'Leaves' have sprouted afresh, and in still greater abundance,"[1] would doubtless have been appalled if he could have known that they would continue to "sprout afresh," growing in abundance if not in "rankness," until the year of the poet's death, 1892. Each successive edition bore the same title, *Leaves of Grass*, with only the date of publication to show that it was a different *Leaves of Grass*. In all, there were nine separate editions (not counting reprints or new issues of an edition) before his death, each different to some extent in content and, until 1881, different also in order and grouping. The order of 1881 was made permanent, but the book continued to grow by "Annexes," so that it is still correct to say that Whitman published or printed nine books which he called without distinction *Leaves of Grass*. It is important, therefore, to know which *Leaves of Grass* a critic has used in making his interpretations and judgments.

These bibliographical facts are especially important in view of Whitman's repeated insistence that he put his own life into his book—he always thought of it as one book. He believed, too, that this book had grown naturally, organically. A friendly critic was representing the poet's view when he stated: "Succeeding editions have the character of expansive growths, like the rings of a tree."[2] Dr. R. M. Bucke, author of the first biography of Whitman under the poet's close supervision, used a different metaphor, but one which also implied consistent and orderly accretion, when he declared of the 1881 edition: "Now it appears before us, perfected, like some grand cathedral that through many years or intervals has grown and grown until the original conception and full design of the architect stand forth."[3]

If *Leaves of Grass* had grown merely by accumulation, in a manner really analogous to the rings of growth on a tree, then the new poems of each edition would record the poet's experiences, states of mind, and progress or retrogression in his artistic development in successive editions. The second edition was almost, though not quite, like this, but subsequent editions were not, for Whitman altered and rearranged his poems in almost every conceivable manner—Mark Van Doren has aptly called it "tinkering" with them.[4] Whitman changed titles, he combined parts of different poems; he revised words, phrases, sentences, whole sections, inserted new lines and passages, grouped and regrouped ceaselessly for twenty-five years.

The year before his death, believing that he had finally achieved the order and form he had worked toward for so many years, Whitman wrote a note for his literary executors:

I place upon you the injunction that whatever may be added [from unpublished poems] to the *Leaves* be supplementary, avowed as such, leaving the book complete as I left it, consecutive to the point I left off, marking always an unmistakable, deep down, unobliterable division line. In the long run the world will do as it pleases with the book. I am determined to have the world know what I was pleased to do.[5]

This wish was carried out, and down to the present time nearly all reprints of *Leaves of Grass* have been the "authorized" text of 1892, often mistakenly called the "deathbed edition." This edition has the merit of being the poet's own final choice of text, but many critics have found that they prefer earlier—usually the first printed—text of major poems, for Whitman's gains in rhythm and elimination of eccentric diction were often at the expense of the vigor, pungency, and originality of his first version. Thus some critics prefer the 1855 version[6] of "Song of Myself" to the better-known 1881 version, while others say that his third edition (1860) was actually his best.[7]

Before discussing Whitman's major poems, therefore, we need some basic information about the contents and characteristics of the nine editions. Of course, for a really thorough study of any given poem, the reader will need the new *Variorum Leaves of Grass*, edited by Sculley Bradley and Harold Blodgett,[8] but a preliminary survey may be useful as an introduction to the bibliographical jungle of Whitman's editions of his *Leaves*.

2

FIRST EDITION(1855): Walt Whitman's first edition of *Leaves of Grass* has always been his most famous, because of its unusual appearance and circumstances of publication as well as the critical furor it stirred up, but until recent years it could be found only in collections of rare books in large institutional libraries or in the private collections of wealthy bibliophiles. It is now available in several inexpensive[9] and one luxury edition,[10] the latter faithfully reproducing the format, binding, and appearance of the original—except that it is printed on better paper and more expertly bound, making it a handsomer book than the original *Leaves*.

Having failed to find a publisher for the poems which he began planning in his 1847 notebook, Whitman decided to have the book printed at his own expense by his friends the Rome Brothers on Fulton Street in Brooklyn. He even set some of the type himself[11] (though not all, as legend has it), had a daguerreotype photograph of himself engraved for a frontispiece, and contracted with a New York bookbinder to make the cover and bind the book. On July 6, 1855, it was advertised for sale at bookstores in Brooklyn and New York City.[12] Whitman himself mailed out review copies, several complimentary copies to prominent authors, including Emerson and Whittier, the former replying with a magnanimous "greeting letter" while the latter is said to have burned his copy.

Even today, the 1855 *Leaves of Grass* is a curious book, with its green cloth cover embossed by ornate leaf and flower designs, its rococo gold-leaf title sprouting unnatural tendrils, roots, branches, and strawberry foliage. In 1855, however, such rococo bindings were not uncommon, and this one was almost an outright imitation of Fanny Fern's contemporary *Fern Leaves*.[13] But when we open this thin quarto of ninety-five pages (plus a nine-page preface) we find more original oddity. As noted before, the title page does not give the name of the

author, but reads simply "LEAVES OF GRASS / Brooklyn, New
York: / 1855." Instead, Whitman used the frontispiece as his
signature—an engraved daguerreotype of himself in shirt
sleeves, in a nonchalant pose. The copyright is in the name of
Walter Whitman. On page 29, line 499, the poet names himself:

> Walt Whitman, an American, one of the roughs, a kosmos,
> Disorderly fleshy and sensual . . . eating drinking and breeding,
> No sentimentalist . . . . no stander above men and women or apart
>   from them . . . . no more modest than immodest.

But if we turn back to that provocative frontispiece, though
the young man in the engraving is nonchalant and unconven-
tional, he does not appear to be rough, disorderly, sensual, or
even fleshy if the word means overweight. His Van Dyke beard
is neatly trimmed, his hat looks like an expensive beaver, and
his genial countenance has a certain air of refinement. The
more one contemplates the image, the more theatrical the pose
seems—this ikon of the "poet of the people" who will "loafe"
and invite his soul and speak in his poems with the voice of a
messiah.

The first item in this odd book is a long, untitled essay
(which came to be known as Whitman's "1855 Preface") on
the nature of the poet America needs, "a bard . . . commensurate with a people." The style is rhapsodic and not unlike the
poems that follow. Whitman never reprinted this essay in its
original form, but he later transposed sentences and even whole
passages from it to several poems, most extensively to "By Blue
Ontario's Shore."[14]

The 1855 edition contains twelve poems without title, except
for the running caption "Leaves of Grass." First comes a poem

of 1336 lines, later called "Song of Myself." It has no section numbers, and each strophe (to use an arbitrary term for the line groupings) is a complete sentence, usually itself composed of independent clauses connected by commas without conjunctions—the clause being the verse unit.

> I celebrate myself,
> And what I assume you shall assume,
> For every atom belonging to me as good belongs to you.

> I loafe and invite my soul,
> I lean and loafe at my ease . . . . observing a spear of summer
>   grass.

> Houses and rooms are full of perfumes . . . . the shelves are
>   crowded with perfumes,
> I breathe the fragrance myself, and know it and like it,
> The distillation would intoxicate me also, but I shall not let it.

The use of periods to mark the caesura or rhetorical pause in a long verse—usually with dramatic effect—is another innovation in the 1855 edition. Both in the Preface and in the poems, the comma is sometimes omitted in a series of nouns or adjectives, as in the line quoted above, "Disorderly fleshy and sensual . . . eating drinking and breeding," with a subtle enlivening effect on rhythm and meaning. Or the conjunction is repeated to stress continuity—read without pause—as in line 1025: "Buying drafts of Osiris and Isis and Belus and Brahma and Adonai . . ." Whitman's experimental use of punctuation (more extensive in the Preface than in the poems) makes one wonder whether the omission of a period at the end of "Song of Myself" was intentional or merely a typographical error. If intentional, the omission might be a symbol of its open-endedness:

Failing to fetch me at first keep encouraged,
Missing me one place search another,
I stop some where waiting for you

The other poems in the 1855 edition are (to give their later titles): "A Song for Occupations," "To Think of Time," "The Sleepers," "I Sing the Body Electric," "Faces," "The Song of the Answerer," "Europe: The 72d and 73d Years of These States," "A Boston Ballad," "There Was a Child Went Forth," "Who Learns My Lesson Complete," and "Great Are the Myths."

Some of these poems are only slightly inferior in artistry to "Song of Myself," notably "To Think of Time," "The Sleepers," and "There Was a Child Went Forth." Two others are in a transition style, and were evidently composed earlier than the final versions of the other '55 poems. "Europe . . . ," an impassioned comment on the failure of the 1848–49 revolutions in Europe, had been published in the New York *Tribune* on June 21, 1850, as "Resurgemus" (Meaning: the martyrs will "live in other young men, O kings, / They live in brothers, again ready to defy you . . ."). "A Boston Ballad" is a satirical, bitterly ironical protest of the arrest in Boston of the escaped slave Anthony Burns, who was returned to his owner in Virginia in June 1854. This poem is almost unique in *Leaves of Grass* (here meaning all editions) in being a satire. The poet tells the mayor sarcastically to send to England for the bones of George III and reinstall them as the ruler of Boston.

The style of "Boston Ballad" would seem to precede the composition of the other poems (except "Europe . . .") by more than a year (to judge by trial *LG* lines in the earlier notebooks), but the satirical purpose may account for the prosodic differences. Here Walt Whitman was playing his political role of the late '40s, not his poetic role of 1855.

In 1959 the poet-critic Malcolm Cowley helped to bring about a new appreciation of the 1855 edition of *Leaves of Grass,* not only by reprinting it in an inexpensive edition but also by his persuasive Introduction. Emerson's "praise of the first edition was unqualified," Cowley wrote, "and it tempts me to make some unqualified statements of my own, as of simple truths that should have been recognized long since."[15]

First statement: that the opening poem, later called "Song of Myself," is Whitman's greatest work, perhaps his one completely realized work, and one of the great poems of modern times. Second, that the other eleven poems of the first edition are not on the same level of realization, but nevertheless are examples of Whitman's freshest and boldest style. At least four of them— their titles in the Deathbed [1892] edition are "To Think of Time," "The Sleepers," "I Sing the Body Electric," and "There Was A Child Went Forth,"—belong in any selection of his best poems. Third, that the text of the first edition is the purest text for "Song of Myself," since many of the later corrections were also corruptions of the style and concealments of the original meaning. Fourth, that it is likewise the best text for most of the other eleven poems, but especially for "The Sleepers"—that fantasia of the unconscious—and "I Sing the Body Electric." And a final statement: that the first edition is a unified work, unlike any later edition, that it gives us a different picture of Whitman's achievement, and that—considering its very small circulation through the years—it might be called the buried masterpiece of American writing ... In the first edition everything belongs together and everything helps to exhibit Whitman at his best, Whitman at his freshest in vision and boldest in language, Whitman transformed by a new experience, so that he wanders among familiar objects and finds that each of them has become a miracle. One can read the book today with something of the amazement and the gratitude for its great power that Emerson felt when reading it more than a century ago.[16]

3

SECOND EDITION (1856): One of the distributors of the 1855 edition of *Leaves of Grass* was the phrenological firm of Fowler and Wells,[17] which also published a popular magazine called *Life Illustrated*. After the printing of the first edition, Whitman became a contributor to this magazine, which in turn publicized his book. This company offered to subsidize a second edition of *Leaves of Grass*, and Whitman began preparing it soon after the appearance of the first. His plans for the new edition were, of course, greatly stimulated by Emerson's letter to him in July 1855. It is even possible that, without this encouragement from a man of Emerson's reputation and prestige, the 1856 edition might never have been undertaken. This letter has become so famous in the history of American literature that it deserves full quotation:

Concord 21 July
Masstts 1855

Dear Sir,

I am not blind to the worth of the wonderful gift of "Leaves of Grass." I find it the most extraordinary piece of wit & wisdom that America has yet contributed. I am very happy in reading it, as great power makes us happy. It meets the demand I am always making of what seemed the sterile & stingy Nature, as if too much handiwork or too much lymph in the temperament were making our western wits fat & mean. I give you joy of your free & brave thought. I have great joy in it. I find incomparable things said incomparably well, as they must be. I find the courage of treatment, which so delights us, & which large perception only can inspire. I greet you at the beginning of a great career, which yet must have had a long foreground somewhere, for such a start. I rubbed my eyes a little to see if this sunbeam were no illusion; but the solid sense of the book is a sobering certainty. It has the best merits, namely, of fortifying & encouraging.

I did not know until I, last night, saw the book advertised in a newspaper, that I could trust the name as real & available for a post-office. I wish to see my benefactor, & have felt much like striking my tasks, & visiting New York to pay you my respects.

R. W. Emerson[18]

Mr. Walter Whitman

Whitman did not reply personally to this generous letter, but he showed it to friends, including Charles Dana, who persuaded him (probably without much difficulty) to permit its publication in the New York *Tribune*, where it appeared on October 10, 1855. For neglecting to ask Emerson's permission, Whitman was severely criticized, and friends of Emerson said that he was displeased, though he never withdrew his endorsement and in subsequent months visited Whitman twice. Whitman made a public reply in an appendix to his second edition, in which he again printed Emerson's letter, followed by his lengthy open letter, dated August 1856: "Here are thirty-two poems, which I send you dear Friend and Master, not having found how I could satisfy myself with any usual acknowledgment of your letter."[19] Whitman then boasts untruthfully that the thousand copies of his first edition "readily sold," and that the new edition is being stereotyped "to print several thousand copies of." Hereafter, "the work of my life is making poems." He then rehearses the familiar arguments for a national literature, and leaves no doubt that he expects to fill the need. Emerson himself was highly critical of contemporary American life, but Whitman more realistically condemns it with the fervor and journalistic flair of a Tom Paine:

> There is no great author [not flattering to Emerson]; everyone has demeaned himself to some etiquette or some impotence. There is no manhood or life-power in poems; there are shoats and geldings more like. Or literature will be dressed up, a fine gentleman, distasteful to our instincts, foreign to our soil. . . . To creeds, literature, art, the army, the navy, the executive, life is hardly proposed, but the sick and dying are proposed to cure the sick and dying. The churches are one vast lie; the people do not believe them, and they do not believe themselves; the priests are continually telling what they know well enough is not so, and keeping back what they know is so. The spectacle is a pitiful one. I think there can never be again upon the festive earth more bad-disordered persons deliberately taking seats, as of late in These States, at the heads of the public tables—such corpses' eyes for judges—such a rascal and thief in the Presidency [Franklin Pierce].[20]

At the time Whitman wrote this open letter to Emerson, he was more concerned with the political situation in his country than with anything else, and when one considers what that situation was, Whitman could hardly be blamed for his concern. The recently organized (1854) Republican Party candidate for the Presidency was John Charles Frémont, the Democratic candidate was James Buchanan, and the former Whig, Millard Fillmore, was running on the Native American ticket (known as the Know-Nothing Party). Whether Whitman sensed that Buchanan would win, he would hardly have been surprised if he had known that President Buchanan's ineptitude would help to bring on a civil war. During that fateful summer of

1856, Whitman also wrote a political pamphlet, called "The Eighteenth Presidency!,"[21] in the same angry tone of much of his letter to Emerson. His warning sounds like some of the maledictions preceding that bizarre Presidential election of 1968:

> To-day, of all the persons in public office in These States, not one in a thousand has been chosen by any spontaneous movement of the people, nor is attending to the interests of the people; all have been nominated and put through by great or small caucuses of the politicians, or appointed as rewards for electioneering; and all consign themselves to personal and party interests. . . . The berths, the Presidency included, are bought, sold, electioneered for, prostituted, and filled with prostitutes.[22]

Whitman was particularly revolted by the debasing of the words "Americanism" by the Know-Nothing Party and "democracy" by the Democrats: "What the so-called democracy are now sworn to perform would eat the faces off the succeeding generations of common people worse than the most horrible disease."[23] He wondered if political parties were not "about played out." He placed "no reliance upon any old party [Democratic], nor upon any new party." He looked for a "Redeemer President," stalwart, incorruptible, emerging from the frontier West, but did not see him anywhere yet. In Europe tyrants trembled, crowns were unsteady, and the human race restive: "No man knows what will happen next, but all know that some such things are to happen as mark the greatest moral convulsions of the earth. Who shall play the hand for America in these tremendous games?"[24]

Believing as he did that the poet must take a very active part in "these tremendous games," Whitman was not inconsistent with his theory in being so preoccupied with politics at the time he wrote his public letter to Emerson, and his intemperate language was not too extreme for the provocation. Both his reply to Emerson and his "Eighteenth Presidency" are also useful in showing the hard-rock realism underlying his idealistic poetic theory and practice.

"Up to the present time," Whitman continued to Emerson, "the people, like a lot of large boys, have no determined tastes, are quite unaware of the grandeur of themselves, and of their destiny, and of their immense strides—accept with voracity whatever is presented them in novels, histories, newspapers, poems, schools, lectures, every thing."[25] America is still "a divine sketch." By calling the sketch "divine," Whitman of course implied that it was destined—as most of the nation believed—to become one of the great nations of the world, practicing genuine liberty and equality, her poets leading the way.

In spite of Whitman's addressing Emerson as "Master," and ending his letter with a pledge to follow in "what you have indicated . . . and enlarge upon it through These States" (the trite language makes us question its sincerity), Whitman's open letter might almost be regarded as a reproach to Emerson for remaining so aloof from contemporary politics and social reforms—the main reason for the alienation of the Young America group from the serene poet-philosopher of Concord.[26] Whitman also affirms this interpretation by devoting several paragraphs to an impassioned denunciation of "the lack of an avowed, empowered, unabashed development of sex" in American art and literature. Whether he has Emerson in mind when he accuses the artists and writers of the nation of belonging to "the neuter gender," he must have been aware that sexual emotion was only discreetly hinted in Emerson's poetry and prose. But what Whitman specifically attacks is legal censorship, which has no relation to Emerson. Although he had not yet suffered from such infringement of his freedom, some of the reviews of his first edition had forewarned him of what to expect.

Here, in his open letter to Emerson, Whitman formally announces his "sex program," and pledges himself to campaign for it:

> By silence or obedience the pens of savans, poets, historians, biographers, and the rest, have long connived at the filthy law and books enslaved to it, that which makes the manhood of a man, that sex, womanhood, maternity, desires, lusty animations, organs, acts, are unmentionable and to be ashamed of, to be driven to skulk out of literature with whatever belongs to them. This filthy law has to be repealed—it stands in the way of great reforms. Of women just as much as men, . . . there should not be infidelism about sex, but perfect faith. Women in These States approach the day of the organic equality with men, without which I see, men cannot have organic equality among themselves. . . . I say that the body of a man or woman, the main matter is so far quite unexpressed in poems; but that the body is to be expressed, and sex is. Of bards for These States, if it comes to a question, it is whether they shall celebrate in poems the eternal decency of the amativeness of Nature, the motherhood of all, or whether they shall be the bards of the fashionable delusion of the inherent nastiness of sex, and the feeble and querulous modesty of deprivation. This is important in poems, because the whole of the other expressions of a nation are but flanges out of its great poems. To me, henceforth, that theory of any thing, no matter what, stagnates in the vitals, cowardly and rotten, while it cannot publicly accept, and publicly name, with specific words, the things on which all existence, all souls, all realization, all decency, all health, all that is worth being here for, all of woman and of man, all beauty, all purity, all friend-

ship, all strength, all life, all immortality depend. The coura-
geous soul, for a year or two to come, may be proved by faith in
sex, and by disdaining concessions.[27]

Of the twenty new poems in the 1856 *Leaves,* less than half a
dozen come specifically within Whitman's new program. And
none of these contains more startlingly sexual imagery than
some of the passages in the 1855 "Song of Myself," and all of
them tend to be more programmatic than personal. None sur-
passes the "Poem of the Body" (the '56 title for the '55 poem,
later retitled "I Sing the Body Electric"), which describes a
"bridal night" in metaphors and rhythms of sexual lyricism
almost unmatched in literature:

> This is the female form!
> A divine nimbus exhales from it from head to foot,
>
> . . . . .
>
> Hair, bosom, hips, bend of legs, negligent falling hands,
>   all diffused—mine too diffused,
> Ebb stung by the flow, and flow stung by the ebb,
>   loveflesh swelling and deliciously aching,
> Limitless limpid jets of love hot and enormous, quivering
>   jelly of love, white-blow and delirious juice,
> Bridegroom-night of love, working surely and safely into
>   the prostrate dawn,
> Undulating into the willing and yielding day,
> Lost in the cleave of the clasping and sweet-fleshed day.

"Poem of Procreation" (later "A Woman Waits for Me") is
more doctrinaire in its theme of "all were lacking, if sex were
lacking, or if the moisture of the right man were lacking," but
what especially offended many contemporary readers was that
the woman waiting sounded like a prostitute. But the sexually

aggressive "I" of the poem drains "the pent-up rivers" of himself into abstract "you women" in order "to start sons and daughters fit for These States." He is a symbolical procreator, like the protagonist of "Bunch Poem" (later "Spontaneous Me"), whose sexual hunger is less erotic than the desire to "saturate what shall produce boys to fill my place when I am through," though the plucking of the "bunch" leaves him with a feeling of "wholesome relief, repose, content." Thus the after-effect of the symbolical orgasm is a healthy relaxation of tension. And perhaps Whitman was right, as also in his satire (his second in *Leaves of Grass*), "Poem on The Proposition of Nakedness," that anyone who distrusts sex and nakedness will also distrust truth, democracy, love, nature, and himself.

These few "sex poems" show progress in Whitman's announced program to Emerson, but in some other respects his second edition makes little advance over his first. The only new poems are scattered, more or less at random, among the old poems, and the collection does not yet have an organized structure. All the poems now have titles, but most of the titles are awkward and some are inappropriate. The initial long poem is called "Poem of Walt Whitman, an American," though the changes do not make it either more personal or more national. His second '55 poem, later called "A Song for Occupations," is entitled "Poem of the Daily Work of the Workmen and Workwomen of These States," and "A Boston Ballad" (later title) is "Poem of Apparitions in Boston, the 78th Year of These States."

In revising lines Whitman is also, as Cowley says,[28] beginning to blur his original bold inspiration. For example, line 52 in the first version of "Song of Myself," which read, "As God comes a loving bedfellow and sleeps at my side all night," is now perverted to a "hugging and loving Bedfellow . . . " But most of the revisions are less significant; the important ones come later.

No poem in the second edition is quite comparable to the '55 "Song of Myself" or "The Sleepers," but this edition does contain the major "Sun-Down Poem" (better known as "Crossing Brooklyn Ferry"). Though most critics recognize it as one of Whitman's masterpieces, it marks a departure from the uncurbed spontaneity of 1855 toward a more controlled, tighter structure, with carefully contrived symbolism. The ferry crossing the East River flowing between two cities carries the poet vicariously into the future, enabling him to share his experience a century hence with his imagined readers. But Whitman's greatest success in this poem, as in his best lines in '55, is visual and tactile, catching the sights and sounds and motions of the river, clouds, sea gulls, people on the ferry and ships at anchor near sundown.

Several other of Whitman's better-known poems first appeared in the second edition, such as "Broad-Axe Poem" ("Song of the Broad-Axe"), "Poem of the Road" ("Song of the Open Road"), and "Poem of Many in One" (finally called "By Blue Ontario's Shore"), the last a reworking of ideas and motifs in the 1855 Preface. But the major importance of this edition is that it shows the direction of Whitman's development, especially his intention to prove his "faith in sex . . . by disdaining concessions." His disdain for public opinion apparently alarmed Fowler and Wells before the completion of the printing of the book, and they kept their names off the title page,[29] so that *Leaves of Grass* again gave the appearance of being privately published. Whitman soon came to feel that he had made a mistake in letting Fowler and Wells have any connection with the book, an unlucky arrangement all around. Even the size and format were unsuitable for his long lines, necessitating runovers that extended to three or four lines of type. The second edition is mainly important as the connecting link between two great editions of *Leaves of Grass*, the first and third.

4

THIRD EDITION (1860): During the four-year interval between the second and third editions of *Leaves of Grass*, a great deal happened to Walt Whitman. For two years (spring of 1857 to summer of 1859) he edited the Brooklyn *Times* and wrote few poems. About this time he became a frequenter of the tap room of Pfaff's bohemian restaurant in New York City, and seems to have formed some homosexual associations. In 1859, unemployed, and his *Leaves of Grass* a commercial failure, he was in low spirits, but in this year he published one of his major poems, "A Child's Reminiscence"—finally, after several experimental titles, becoming the melodious "Out of the Cradle Endlessly Rocking."[30] This poem is allegorical, like "Crossing Brooklyn Ferry," though with a more pronounced story line and more expressive symbolical imagery, rhythm, and even syntax. Long regarded as an elegy, it is now usually interpreted as a symbolical account of how the little boy listening to a mocking bird lament the loss of its mate became a man and a poet, a "solitary singer" himself, the burden of whose songs would be "unsatisfied love." Called "A Word Out of the Sea" in 1860, this is the first new poem in the third edition.

The publication of a new edition became possible for Whitman when Thayer and Eldridge, a young but highly respected publishing firm in Boston, suddenly offered in the spring of 1860 to become his publishers.[31] Whitman prepared the new book with care and supervised the printing in Boston. Unfortunately, Thayer and Eldridge went into bankruptcy the following year, but before then *Leaves of Grass* did get professionally published and for a short time circulated. The book was a thick volume (octavo) bound in cloth, with 456 well-printed pages on good paper. For the frontispiece, Whitman used an engraving of a portrait painted by Charles Hine which shows him in a highly stylized pose, with short beard, Byronic collar, and Windsor tie looped in a huge loose bow. This portrait looks more like a Victor Hugo than like the poet of American democracy.

In recent years this third edition has come to be regarded by a few critics as one of Whitman's most important. In 1933 the Danish critic Frederik Schyberg in his *Walt Whitman*[32] called it the "most revealing" (autobiographically) of all editions of *Leaves of Grass*, containing evidence of a recent, almost tragic, moral and emotional crisis, and declared the "Calamus" poems Whitman's only real love poems. The poet's inner struggle, Schyberg thought, was also a curious parallel to the social and political turmoil that would soon divide his nation in the greatest civil war in history. Schyberg's interpretations were summarized in my *Walt Whitman Handbook* (1946) and gained some currency in America before the Danish book was translated into English.[33]

The importance of the third edition has been fully evaluated by Roy Harvey Pearce in his Introduction to a facsimile edition of the 1860 text (1961). Pearce is less interested in the poet's emotional experiences than in his poetic development. Specifically, Pearce believes that Whitman discovered in this edition just how far he could go with language, "only to discover that he could go no farther. Such a discovery constitutes the principal element of greatness in the 1860 *Leaves of Grass*. I suggest that it is at least worth entertaining the notion that such a discovery constitutes the principal element of greatness in Whitman's poetry as a whole."[34]

Pearce's analysis is subtle and difficult to summarize briefly without misrepresentation, but his major point is that the 1860 edition was a "turning point" in the growth of *Leaves of Grass*. In subsequent editions Whitman abandoned the exploration of himself—that is, himself as a poet, what it means to create a poem—and became (or tried to become) a prophetic or "mythic" poet. As D. H. Lawrence charged, he "mentalized" his poems.[35] In 1860 his "Enfans d'Adam" and "Calamus" sequences are not so much the record of his own sexual ambivalence (though that is implicit) as "analogies" by which Whitman attempted to teach his readers "all that is involved in moving from sexuality to love." Pearce has a valid point, for in the 1860 "Enfans d'Adam" and "Calamus" Whitman attempts more than the carrying out of his program of sexual honesty announced in 1856; he also presents artistic creations as analogous to sexual procreation and anticipates Freud in finding that the two are vitally interrelated. Other critics, Schyberg especially, have seen these poems as sublimations of Whitman's unsatisfied "procreant urge." But whatever the interpretation of Whitman's necessity, the record of his great experiment in expression is in this third edition of *Leaves of Grass*.

In 1860 for the first time Whitman began organizing his book on an archetypal plan. Though he retained all the poems of his two previous editions, he rearranged them, with revisions and changes of title, so that, he hoped, they would give meaning to each other. First comes a new poem, "Proto-Leaf," meaning (in the context of the new arrangement) not only *first* or introductory but also *prototype*. As in his 1855 Preface, Whitman announces his program to "strike up for a new world." The later title for this poem, "Starting from Paumanok," suggests that it is biographical—about the poet born on Long Island, which the Indians called Paumanok—but the 1860 title is better; the Paumanoker is archetypal:

> This then is life,
> Here is what has come to the surface after so many
>   throes and convulsions.

There is, however, a tension in the 1860 version (even an outright conflict in the earlier manuscript version edited by Fredson Bowers)[36] between the poet's public and private roles. First he "will be the bard of Personality," a prototype American democratic personality. In the manuscript version he then renounces this role to become a passionate lover of one person (a man), and even in the published poem (1860) the poet sings "companionship" with an overemphatic pathos ("O you and me at last—and us two only . . ."). But he also seriously proposes that a democratic society rests on love, and not only "Proto-Leaf" but every poem of his will be "an evangel-poem of comrades and of love."

The second poem in the third edition is "Walt Whitman" ("Song of Myself") slightly revised, an illustration not so much of the poet's actual self as of the ideal self of his envisioned "Democracy for These States." Then, as if further illustrating and developing this theme, comes a new group (containing both new and old poems) called "Chants Democratic and Native American." The sequence begins with a fortissimo overture "Apostrophe," which rehearses every aspect of Whitman's nationalistic poetic program with such inflated rhetoric that it soon becomes tiresome to the reader, and Whitman had the good judgment to drop it in all future editions.

The twenty-one poems in "Chants Democratic" are numbered instead of titled, beginning with three poems from the second edition, "Poem of Many in One" (adapted from the '55 Preface, "A nation announcing itself . . . ," etc.); then the "Broad-Axe Poem" as number 2—the "shapes arise" . . . ; and "Poem of Daily Workmen . . ." as number 3. The last is embarrassingly sentimental, with the poet's appeal to his readers to "Push closer, my lovers, and take the best I possess," but he is consistent in maintaining that "All I love America for, is contained in men and women like you." The remaining poems in this group, both old and new, support this theme in one way or another. Poem number 21 ends with the assertion that "the visions of poets" are the most solid realities for the nation:

> Democracy rests finally upon us, (I, my brethren, begin it,)
> And our visions sweep through eternity.

The next group is called simply "Leaves of Grass," with a pun on *leaves*, each leaf being a poem, an experience. (In "Song of Myself" he had called the grass "the flag of my disposition, out of green stuff woven.") Leaf number 1 is the poem Whitman had published in the April 1860 issue of the *Atlantic Monthly* as "Bardic Symbols" (later "As I Ebbed with the Ocean of Life").[37] The earlier title plainly labels this poem as the autobiography of a poet. What it tells primarily is his discouragement and self-doubt during his "ebb" years (between his second and third editions), when he felt himself to be a castaway on the beach, mocked by his earlier poetic ambitions. But now in humility and despair he understands the "moaning" of the "fierce old mother," the ocean, symbol of death but also of maternity and implied rebirth. Even though the poet envisions his death in lines which James Russell Lowell refused to print in the *Atlantic* ("See! from my dead lips the ooze exuding at last! / See—the prismatic colors, glistening and rolling!"),[38] he knows that he is going through a natural cycle of ebb and flow in his life as a poet, and that the "flow" will return.

This group does not trace Whitman's spiritual biography in any systematic order, but in general the poems reveal his struggles to become the archetypal poet. In number 10 he announces: "It is ended—I dally no more"; he will inure himself to hardships and press on with his great work as an artist,

> Not to chisel ornaments,
> But to chisel with free stroke the heads and limbs of
>   plenteous Supreme Gods, that The States may
>   realize them, walking and talking.

The final "leaf" in this group (No. 24) discloses the ultimate effect Whitman hopes to accomplish in his poems, a miraculous transubstantiation of his words made flesh:

> What you are holding is in reality no book, nor part of a book,
> It is a man, flushed and full-blooded—it is I—So long!

So real is this illusion that the poet asks his reader "to take from my lips this kiss / Whoever you are, I give it especially to you . . ." (One paradox of this fantasy-contact is that the poet wants each of his many readers to feel that he speaks to him or her alone.) However the reader may react to this vicarious intimacy, Whitman was testing how far he could go in making love to his readers by means of words (Pearce's thesis). And the curious thing is how many have felt the emotional tug, women as well as men, some of whom actually wrote love letters to Whitman—to his embarrassment, for he had no desire to exchange his fantasy love-making for the act.

To a critical mind the question that arises is: What does this have to do with creating an archetypal personality for American democracy? To Whitman, evidently, everything, because his democracy was a spiritual ideal, and the practitioners were to be religious devotees more than political activists. In an earlier notebook he had referred to his projected *Leaves of Grass* as a "New Bible for Democracy,"[39] and in his 1855 Preface he had announced that "There will soon be no more priests" and "prophets en masse shall take their place."

One of these "prophets en masse" was the poet of the next poem in the third edition, "Salut au Monde" ("Poem of Salutations" in 1856), which is a poem of worship of both the outer (physical) and the inner (mental, spiritual) worlds. The burden of its message to the acolytes is: explore your own inner space, until you know it matches the wonders of the natural world. In a "divine rapport" the poet's spirit circles the earth and finds "equals and lovers . . . in all lands." Appropriately, "Poem of Joys" comes next, and then "A Word Out of the Sea" (the 1859 "A Child's Reminiscence"). The word the sea whispers is "death," the necessary link, as Lucretius had taught, in the cycle of birth, life, death, and return. Next comes "Leaf of Faces," a logical place for this 1855 poem because human faces are windows for the immortal soul:

> In each house is the ovum—it comes forth after a
>   thousand years.

> Spots or cracks at the windows do not disturb me,
> Tall and sufficient stand behind, and make signs to me,
> I read the promise, and patiently wait.

This seems to be Whitman's adaptation of the Hindu doctrine of transmigration. In one generation the soul may be housed in a defective body, but "in a score or two of years" the "real landlord" will appear, for "The Lord advances, and yet advances . . ." The import of this poem is: have patience with defective persons; their souls will be reborn in bodies nearer perfection. In fact, this is a religious poem, and the remainder of the third edition supports the idea that in this book Whitman was trying to create his "New Bible."

Whitman's intention has often been misunderstood because he was not in any literal sense trying to replace the Hebraic-Christian Bible, or even to parallel it in the structure and contents of his "New Bible." But the message he is trying to convey by the arrangement of his poems and his group titles is that all physical life rests on an unseen but strongly felt spiritual world (a major doctrine of the American Transcendentalists), that man's worship of this world should be expressed by his ecstatic joy in its beauty and pleasures, especially sexual ones, which bring human beings closest to their eternal sources. Schyberg has compared Whitman's religion to the Hasidic worship through joy, and the analogy is apt.

Hasidic joy is especially apparent in "Enfans d'Adam." In the garden which is the world the poet finds ". . . all beautiful to me—all wondrous, / My limbs, and the quivering fire that ever plays through them . . ." He sings (No. 2) "the phallus" and "the song of procreation," not only as a duty but also as a means of worshipping the miraculous life-force, which is the soul ever seeking a physical outlet or embodiment. At times the "I" of the poem seems almost to be this soul or immortal self, but it is also the poet trying to find words to express his adoration—"I . . . delirate" he says in number 12. In number 14 he "aches with love," and asks, "Does not all matter, aching, attract matter?" His final words in "Enfans d'Adam" are: "Be not afraid of my body." That is, any body, all bodies. They and all their functions are God-given.

The connecting poems between "Enfans d'Adam" and "Calamus" emphasize this theme of worshipping the spiritual source through joy in its outlets:

> I am larger than I thought,
> I did not know I held so much goodness.
> All seems beautiful to me,
> I can repeat over to men and women, You have done such
>   good to me, I would do the same to you.
> I will recruit myself and you as I go,
> I scatter myself among men and women as I go,
> I will toss the new gladness and roughness among them;
> Whoever denies me, it shall not trouble me,
> Whoever accepts me, he or she shall be blessed and
>   shall bless me.

And here is the test of "wisdom":

> Wisdom is of the Soul, is not susceptible of proof,
>   is its own proof,
> Applies to all stages and objects and qualities, and
>   is content,
> Is the certainty of the reality and immortality of
>   things, and the excellence of things;
> Something there is in the float of the sight of things
>   that provokes it out of the Soul.

"To the Sayers of Words" ("Song of the Rolling Earth"), the next poem, is almost a variation on the same theme of wisdom inherent in natural objects. Words are *in things*, not in printed or written symbols: " . . . the substantial words are in the ground and sea, / They are in the air—they are in you."

I swear I begin to see little or nothing in audible words!
I swear I think all merges toward the presentation of
   the unspoken meanings of the earth!
Toward him who sings the songs of the body, and of the
   truths of the earth . . .

The group of forty-five poems called "Calamus" in 1860 has come to be regarded as Whitman's homosexual love poems. And they are in general on the theme of "manly attachment," love of comrades, male friendship, etc. The pink root of the calamus plant (or sweet flag) is a token passed around among the members of an esoteric cult. The token might be said to have religious symbolism, and in a vague sense this is true. The exchange of the token binds the comrades in an unspoken compact so exclusive between two persons and held in such shyness and secrecy that it is not the worshipping of a divine power through erotic ecstasy, as in "Enfans d'Adam," but simply eroticism for its own sake. Yet at times, as in poem number 34, the poet's search for "lovers" (No. 33) leads him to dream of an invincible city of friends. Finally, however, the poet's "Calamus" emotions are satisfied (No. 45) in the fantasy that "a century hence" he will become the "lover" of unseen readers. No doubt the similarity of this motif to the theme of the 1856 poem now (1860) called "Crossing Brooklyn Ferry" led Whitman to place this poem at the end of "Calamus." Yet what is so remarkable about the "Calamus" poems is not their theme and place in the "New Bible," but their sustained lyricism. They vibrate with deep personal emotion, and some of them rank very high among the great love poems in world literature, though the love is not traditional heterosexual love.

The remaining poems in the third edition are mostly short, especially the new ones. A group called "Messenger Leaves" revives the "New Bible" connotations, especially in the first poem, "To Him that Was Crucified," in which the poet addresses Christ (not actually named) as "dear brother" and "my comrade." The predominant theme of these poems is the place of the individual in time and eternity, as in the '56 "Sleep-Chasings" ("The Sleepers") and "Burial" (a '55 poem later called "To Think of Time"). In the final poem of the book, "So Long," the poet envisions himself, as in the final poem of "Calamus" (which was at one time evidently intended to end the edition), as a disembodied spirit living in his poems, still in future ages exchanging kisses with his readers:

> Remember my words—I love you—I depart from materials,
> I am as one disembodied, triumphant, dead.

In all subsequent editions "So Long" was retained as the terminal poem, a kind of benediction, but it was never again so appropriate as in the 1860 *Leaves of Grass*.

5

Walt Whitman was evidently not aware how nearly he had come to producing a unified book in 1860. He could have simplified the task of his later critics, and perhaps even of ordinary readers, if he had let his *Leaves of Grass* remain in the 1860 version. He could then have started a new collection of poems with new themes and the emotions which he experienced during the Civil War and its aftermath. Possibly if Thayer and Eldridge could have kept this edition in print, Whitman might have followed this strategy, for before their bankruptcy they began advertising a second book of poems by Whitman to be called *Banner at Day-Break*, to contain about two hundred pages.[40] The title poem of the book-to-be was not one of

Whitman's better compositions and he later abandoned it, but it sounded a new note in his poetic nationalism—ardently patriotic and idealizing war in defense of the nation. Had it not been announced in the summer of 1860, we would think this poem expressed Whitman's reaction to Lincoln's call for volunteers to save the Union, but possibly the Lincoln-Douglas debates in 1858 had given Whitman a foreboding of the impending crisis. The point is that he was now responding more immediately to contemporary events than in most of his poems in the first three editions of *Leaves of Grass*.

Another poem announced for inclusion in *Banner at Day-Break* was so immediate that it could be called an occasional poem. This was "Errand Bearers," published in *The New York Times* on June 27, 1860, on the occasion of the visit of the Japanese envoys to New York City on June 16, when they were honored by a mammoth parade up Broadway.[41] Whitman himself witnessed the parade and wrote the poem before his excitement cooled.

> Over sea, hither from Niphon,
> Courteous, the Princes of Asia, swart-cheeked princes,
> First-comers, guests, two-sworded princes,
> Lesson-giving princes, leaning back in their open
>   barouches, bare-headed, impassive,
> This day they ride through Manhattan.
>
>   .   .   .   .   .
>
> When million-footed Manhattan, unpent, descends to
>   its pavements,
> When the thunder-cracking guns arouse me with the proud
>   roar I love,
>
>   .   .   .   .   .
>
> When the answer that waited thousands of years, answers,
> I too, arising, answering, descend to the pavements,
>   merge with the crowd, and gaze with them.

The Japanese princes had come to the United States to negotiate a treaty after Commodore Perry had forced an end to Japan's "closed door" policy.[42] Whitman looked upon their visit as the beginning of a new era of communication between Orient and Occident, when peoples and cultures would mingle with practical benefits to both. But also as an extension of "Libertad"—though a century later it would be called Americanization.

The other important poem announced for *Banner at Day-Break* was "Quadrel," an early title for "Chanting the Square Deific,"[43] not published until 1865, but in preparation (as notebooks show)[44] before the 1855 *Leaves*. For the Christian Trinity Whitman would substitute a Quaternity, representing (1) law and authority (as in Jehovah, Brahma, Saturnius, Kronos); (2) love, compassion (as in Christ, Hermes, Hercules); (3) pride, revolt against the God-head (Satan); (4) the pervading, mediating life-principle, "Santa Spirita."[45] This is the most theological of all Whitman's poems, and was perhaps to have had a place in the 1860 "New Bible" but could not be completed in time. By 1867 (the fourth edition of *Leaves of Grass*) the dream of a "New Bible" had faded, though a religious motif had not.

The bankruptcy of Thayer and Eldridge and the distractions of the Civil War had aborted the publication of *Banner at Day-Break*, and by the time Whitman could resume publication of his poems at the end of the war, he was a different poet, who had either forgotten or was unable to carry out his prewar plans. However, the hiatus in publication did not mean that he took a holiday from his poems. He wrote and planned continuously. Even before that fateful April 13, 1861, he had begun composing some of the poems which he later published in *Drum-Taps*. At the outbreak of the war he wrote a "recruiting"

poem, "Beat! Beat! Drums!",[46] and responded excitedly to the
patriotic fervor which swept the North.

On his forty-second birthday (May 31, 1861) Whitman composed a new preface for a fourth edition of his poems. He had
no prospects of publishing a new edition—and soon the dis-
rupted economy of the nation would make such a prospect
even more remote—but we can see from this manuscript that
Whitman was now committed once more to expanding and per-
fecting his one book instead of writing new (separate) ones.
His basic ideas had changed little since his 1855 Preface, but his
earlier confidence was giving way to the conviction that the
most he could do was to suggest and initiate. "The paths to the
house are made," he wrote in 1861 for his tentative new preface, "—but where is the house itself?"

> Dear friend! not here for you, melodious narratives, no pictures
> here, for you to con at leisure, as bright creations all outside
> yourself. But of SUGGESTIVENESS, with new centripetal reference
> out of the miracles of every day, this is the song—naught made
> complete by me for you, but only hinted to be made by you by
> robust exercise. I have not done the work and cannot do it. But
> you must do the work and make what is within the following
> song.[47]

This is a provocative theory of poetic ontology, yet it betrays
the poet's lack of confidence in his creation. Ultimately the life
of every poem is in the response of readers to it, but Whitman
is saying that he only provides the materials out of which each
reader must construct his own poem.

In another manuscript preface[48] on which Whitman noted
"Dec. 23, 1864 / *good & must be used,*" he enumerated the
"ideas" he hoped to inculcate in his poems: (1) "sacredness of
the individual"; (2) "the idea of love" to fuse and combine

"the whole"; (3) religion—"purifying all things, gives endless direction and growth to a man or woman . . ." But this is little more than intellectual doodling. If it signifies anything, it is that Whitman was beset by doubt, dissatisfaction, and a feeling of having fallen far short of his dream of himself as the "American poet" of 1855. As a consequence, he would spend the remainder of his life reshuffling and rewriting his poems in the vain attempt to give them some transcendent symbolical meaning and allegorical order.

The effects of the Civil War on Whitman's continuation of his *Leaves of Grass* are most dramatically apparent in his revisions of the third edition in a copy which he called his "Blue Book"[49] because he had protected it with a blue wrapper. He left it in Brooklyn with his mother while he remained in Washington visiting the war hospitals, dispensing cheer and small gifts to the soldiers, but he took it with him to the capital when he returned in January 1865 to work as a "clerk" in the Department of the Interior, and kept it in his desk. One evening after work hours, someone removed this copy and showed it to the ex-Methodist minister who was the Secretary, James Harlan, who promptly dismissed Whitman on a trumped-up charge.[50] Friends came to the poet's rescue and he was given employment in the Attorney General's office, but controversy over the method of his removal from the Department of the Interior would rage and rumble for years to come.

Some critics and biographers have thought that Whitman was actually deleting obscene passages in his third edition— "toning down" the text—and that in this marked copy he accidentally called them to the attention of his snooping employer. However, Professor Arthur Golden in his judicious Introduction to his recent edition of the "Blue Book" points out that this was not true. Whitman's deletions were primarily for improvement of style and elimination of unnecessary repetitions.[51] He did mark "out for revision" "Calamus" poems 8, 9, 10, 12, 32, 37, and 38. Two of these (8 and 9) and one not marked for deletion (11) were never again reprinted in *Leaves of Grass*. Since they are almost, if not actually, the finest lyrics in the original "Calamus" group, they did not need revision for style or structure—and Whitman's judgment for such needs was usually sound. Probably Whitman realized that they revealed too much of his private life. Number 8 was especially autobiographical: "Long I thought that knowledge alone would suffice me . . ." First he had wanted to rival the deeds of "dauntless persons" in the novels and epics he had read in his youth. The next stage of his ambitions was "to strike up the songs of the New World—And then I believed my life must be spent in singing . . ." (his state of mind in 1855–56). But now (1860) he gives notice to his country that

> . . . I can be your singer of songs no longer—One who
> loves me is jealous of me, and withdraws me from all
> but love,
> With the rest I dispense—I sever from what I thought would
> suffice me, for it does not—it is now empty and
> tasteless to me,
> I heed knowledge, and the grandeur of The States, and the
> example of heroes, no more.

In no other single poem or group of poems did Whitman ever make such a clear confession of his unstable ambitions. In number 9 the poet has lost his lover and is "sore and heavy-hearted." He is forgotten, but he can never forget. He is ashamed of his torment, "but it is useless—I am what I am," and he wonders "if other men ever have the like, out of the like feelings?" But not all of these homosexual love poems show such despondency or sense of guilt. Number 11, which Whitman did not mark in his "Blue Book" for deletion, was his finest love lyric, and must be quoted in full to illustrate its beauty and power:

When I heard of the plaudits given to my name in the capital,*
Still it was not a happy night for me that followed;
And else, when I caroused, or when my plans were accomplished,
    still I was not happy;
But the day when I rose at dawn from the bed of perfect health,
    refreshed, singing, inhaling the ripe breath of autumn,
When I saw the full moon in the west grow pale and disappear
    in the morning light,
When I wandered alone over the beach, and, undressing, bathed,
    laughing with the cool waters, and saw the sun rise,
And when I thought how my dear friend, my lover, was on his
    way coming, O then I was happy;
O then each breath tasted sweeter—and all that day my food
    nourished me more—And the beautiful day passed well,
And the next came with equal joy—And with the next, at
    evening, came my friend;
And that night, while all was still, I heard the waters
    roll slowly continually up the shores,
I heard the hissing rustle of the liquid and sands,†
    whispering, to congratulate me,
For the one I love most lay sleeping by me under the
    same cover in the cool night,
In the stillness, in the autumn moonbeams, his face was
    inclined toward me,
And his arm lay lightly around my breast—And that night
    I was happy.

* Deleted: "at the close of the day how my name / had been received with plaudits," but restored in 1867.
† Deleted: "as directed to me."

Whatever the reader's reaction may be to Whitman's homo-
erotic emotions, this "Calamus" poem reveals the passional life
of a real person, not the lofty idealism of an archetypal poet-
prophet. But Whitman apparently realized that the "I" of this
poem was so real as to undercut his mythic "I"; for it was the
mythic role that he wished to emphasize in his next edition.
The book would begin with his 1860 "Proto-Leaf," but with
the more personal title of "Starting from Paumanok," and long,
rhythmical lines that would *sound* the poet's heroic character.
Although the new version does idealize the poet's background,
the difference is not so much in the ideas as in the space
imagery and soaring movement of the revision. In 1860 "Proto-
Leaf" began:

Free, fresh, savage,
Fluent, luxuriant, self-contained, fond of persons and places,
Fond of fish-shape Paumanok, where I was born . . .

The revised poem began:

Starting from fish-shape Paumanok, where I was born,
Well-begotten, and raised by a perfect mother,
After roaming many lands—lover of populous pavements,
Dweller in Mannahatta, city of ships, my city, or
    on southern savannas,
Or a soldier camped, or carrying my knapsack and gun . . .

In succeeding lines many other places are visited in imagination, giving this new introduction to *Leaves of Grass* a conti-
nental sweep, and also suggesting Whitman's serious intention
to revise and arrange his poems to help unite his war-torn country, North and South. This would likewise be a theme in his
Drum-Taps poems, which he would add to his new edition
after first publishing them separately. He was also inserting

some new passages into "Song of Myself" (still called "Walt Whitman") to make this 1855 poem reflect the meaning of the war. For example, the passage on the integrity of the *self* in the midst of external events, distractions, disappointments, etc. (sec. 19 in 1860), he interpolated in the "Blue Book" copy:[52]

> Battles, the horrors of fratricidal war, the fever of
>   doubtful news, the fitful events,

before the 1860 lines:

> These come to me days and nights, and go from me again,
> But they are not the Me myself.

Then in section 341 in a passage on his associations with the mechanic, the woodman, the farm-boy, fishermen, and seamen, Whitman added:

> The soldier camp'd or in battle, or on the march is mine,
> On the night ere the pending battle many seek me, & I do
>   not fail them
> On that solemn night (it may be the last,) those that
>   know me seek me.

Although Whitman's new edition would be his most nationalistic, he revised his "Chants Democratic" so extensively that he finally eliminated the group title and redistributed the poems in 1867. Chant number 1 ("A nation announcing itself ...") he remotivated by such insertions as these:

> As I wandered the Prairies alone at night,
> (As I mused of these mighty days & of peace returned,
>   and the dead that return no more,)
> A phantom, gigantic, superb, with stern visage, arrested me,

Chant me a poem, it said, *that breathes my native air alone,*
Chant me a song of *the throes of Democracy;*
(Democracy, the destined conqueror—yet treacherous
   lip-smiles every where,
And death and infidelity at every step,)

In a longer insertion Whitman penned an invocation to
"Libertad," with her foot on the neck of the "Scorner,"

The menacing, arrogant one, that strode & advanced with
   his senseless scorn, bearing the murderous knife:
Lo! the wide swelling one, the braggart that would
   yesterday do so much!
Already carrion dead & despised of all the earth—an offal rank,
This day to the dunghill maggots spurn'd.

These strong words were not vindicative gloating over the
defeat of the Confederacy, but rather praise of the Union for
having kept Democracy alive. Whitman would never again
(except in his fourth edition) be so shrilly patriotic and at
times even chauvinistic in his scorn of foreign nations, doubtless because many of them (England, especially) had sympa-
thized with the Confederacy. He was isolationist because his
nation had had to stand alone in her darkest hour, and had survived. Several of the longer "Chants" and some of the 1860
"Leaves of Grass" group he marked for a new group to be
called "Pioneers," evidently intending by this word not only to
honor the frontier settlers but also to symbolize the American
spirit of courage and perseverance in the democratic dream.

6

DRUM-TAPS (1865): Near the end of March 1865, Walt Whitman obtained a three-week leave from his government position

in Washington to be with his brother George, who had returned to Brooklyn after release from a Confederate prison.[53] During this time Walt arranged for the printing of his *Drum-Taps*. Like almost everyone else in the North, he was expecting the war to end any day, and on April 9 Lee did surrender at Appomattox Court House, and three days later the capital of the Confederacy at Montgomery, Alabama, capitulated. It seemed almost prophetic that Whitman should just then be giving his wartime poems to the printer. But the national tragedy had not ended, for on April 14, Good Friday, President Lincoln was assassinated. Now *Drum-Taps* could not be regarded as finished. But Whitman let the printing continue anyway, though he managed to insert a hastily written elegy, "Hush'd Be the Camps To-day," to commemorate the funeral of Lincoln in Washington on April 19.

The first issue of *Drum-Taps* was a hastily compiled little book of only seventy-two pages, not even containing all of Whitman's war poems, such as "Dirge for Two Veterans," a poem that in future years would often be set to music. Paper was still scarce, and the printer had advised Whitman to wait for a decline in prices and an increase in quality and quantity, but Whitman was impatient to get the book printed. No doubt he withheld some poems in order to reduce the cost of printing and paper, yet he included several poems from the abortive *Banner at Day-Break*: the title poem now called "Song of the Banner at Day-Break," "The Centenarian's Story" (originally "Washington's First Battle," not a Civil War subject but a patriotic one), and "A Broadway Pageant."

The poems in *Drum-Taps* had no chronological order (either in historical subject matter or in date of composition), and the book had only a faint thematic structure, beginning with a paean to Manhattan as a prelude,

Lightly strike on the stretch'd typaneum, pride
   and joy in my city,
How she led the rest to arms . . .

and two poems as epilogue. In the first of these, "Pensive on Her Dead Gazing, I Heard the Mother of All," Mother Nature prays to the earth to absorb her "young men's beautiful bodies" and their "precious blood," to be given back in "unseen essence and odor . . . centuries hence." The final poem is the poet's prideful apology:

Not youth pertains to me,
Nor delicatesse—I cannot beguile the time with talk;
Awkward in the parlor, neither a dancer nor elegant;
In the learn'd coterie sitting constrain'd and still—
   for learning inures not to me;
Beauty, knowledge, fortune, inure not to me—yet there
   are things inure to me;
I have nourish'd the wounded, and sooth'd many a dying
   soldier;
And at intervals I have strung together a few songs,
Fit for war, and the life of the camp.

From the time Whitman visited his wounded brother George in Virginia in the spring of 1862 until the end of the war, except for intervals of his own illness, he had visited thousands of soldiers in army hospitals, dispensing little gifts but most of all dispensing his sympathy and understanding to wounded and discouraged men. Occasionally he served as a volunteer nurse. A poem called "The Dresser" (later "The Wound-Dresser") gives the impression that Whitman's services were primarily those of nurse on the battlefield and field hospital. Actually he never served on the battlefield or in the field hospitals but in the hospitals in and near Washington, where he sometimes stayed with a soldier during an operation and tended him afterward. But the poem need not be taken as literal autobiography. It effectively dramatizes the work of the male nurse during the war, and the emotion is genuine. In lines interpolated in 1871, Whitman accurately traces his changing attitude as the war progressed and states his actual role in it:

> (Arous'd and angry, I'd thought to beat the alarum,
>   and urge relentless war,
> But soon my fingers fail'd me, my face droop'd and
>   I resign'd myself,
> To sit by the wounded and soothe them, or silently
>   watch the dead:) . . .

In form as well as content, the *Drum-Taps* poems are a sharp departure from the bold experiments in the first three editions of *Leaves of Grass*—especially the first. The poems are briefer (fifty-three in seventy-two pages) and stylistically much nearer contemporary Victorian verse than Whitman's earlier poems. They have personifications (the speaking "banner," the praying "Mother of All," the prophetic voice in "Over the Carnage . . ."); they have visions (*cf.* "The Veteran's Vision") and other stock devices. "Pioneers! O Pioneers!" is even in rhyme, meter (basically trochaic), and stanza with a refrain. The language is exclamatory, often artificially excited, with many inversions (predicate-subject, noun-adjective) and conventional contractions (*o'er, well-grey'd hair, trellis'd grape*). Neo-classic poets had used these contractions for the sake of meter (though sometimes only for the eye, as Whitman's *'d* often is, too; *e.g.*, *grey'd* and *trellis'd*, in which the *e* is not pronounced in normal speech) and Whitman did not need them for this purpose. But he apparently felt that these ancient conventions made his

poems sound and look more like poetry; he declared with pride
that his *Drum-Taps* was more artistic than *Leaves of Grass*.

Yet the artificial prosody of *Drum-Taps* is not an indication
of insincerity, and even poems like "Come up from the Fields
Father"—"to hear a letter from our Pete," fatally wounded—
are genuinely moving in their homely details of the pathos and
tragedy of war. And the almost metrical rhythms of the
Drum-Taps verse are not inappropriate for poems about march-
ing men, beating drums, the call of bugles, and military rou-
tines. A typical example of the artful style, too obvious symbolism, heavy pathos, and yet somehow convincing evocation of a
common scene in the war is "A Sight in Camp in the Day-
Break Grey and Dim" (note the effect of the inversions on the
rhythm):

A sight in camp in the day-break grey and dim,
As from my tent I emerge so early, sleepless,
As slow I walk in the cool fresh air, the path
    near by the hospital-tent,
Three forms I see on stretchers lying, brought
    out there, untended lying,
Over each the blanket spread, ample brownish woolen
    blanket,
Grey and heavy blanket, folding, covering all.

Curious, I halt, and silent stand;
Then with light fingers I from the face of the
    nearest, the first just lift the blanket:
Who are you, elderly man so gaunt and grim, with well-
    grey'd hair, and flesh all sunken about the eyes?
Who are you, my dear comrade?

Then to the second I step—And who are you, my child
    and darling?
Who are you, sweet boy, with cheeks yet blooming?

Then to the third—a face nor child, nor old, very
    calm, as of beautiful yellow-white ivory:
Young man, I think I know you—I think this face of
    yours is the face of the Christ himself;
Dead and divine, and brother of all, and here again
    he lies.

By late summer in 1865 Whitman had completed his great
elegy on President Lincoln, "When Lilacs Last in the Dooryard
Bloom'd," which Swinburne called "the most sweet and sonorous nocturne ever chanted in the church of the world."[54]
With this as his chief new poem, Whitman then had a *Sequel
to Drum-Taps* printed in Washington, D.C. This made a pamphlet of only twenty-four pages, but by adding it to the
unbound sheets of *Drum-Taps* printed in New York the previous spring, Whitman had a more impressive second issue of
Drum-Taps ready for distribution in December of 1865.

All the eighteen new poems were short except "Lilacs," and
they were a mixed lot—as in *Drum-Taps,* not all war poems,
such as "Chanting the Square Deific." But the *Sequel* also contained "Captain! My Captain!", soon to become and remain
Whitman's most famous poem. It is quite untypical of him,
being (like "Pioneers! O Pioneers!" in *Drum-Taps*) in rhyme,
meter, and stanzas with a refrain.

O captain! my captain! our fearful trip is done;

. . . . .

    Where on the deck my captain lies
        Fallen cold and dead.

The symbolism is trite, the iambic-anapestic movement artificial, and the rhymes erratic, but thousands of school children
have found the poem easy to memorize and recite—usually in a
singsong tone. It is fair to say that Whitman, like Poe, is best

known for his worst poem, but it shows the kind of popular success he might have had if he had let himself descend to this level.

"Dirge for Two Veterans" also has metrical rhythm and conventional stanza form, but the rhythm, the simple imagery, and the theme are in perfect accord:

> I hear the great drums pounding,
> And the small drums steady whirring;
> And every blow of the great convulsive drums,
>   Strikes me through and through.

But the *Sequel* was a literary landmark in American literature because it contained the great "Lilacs" elegy. (For critical interpretation, see Chapter V.) Even this poem lacks the sharp imagery and daring language of "Song of Myself," and it makes extensive use of the pastoral motifs and symbolical nature images of the elegiac tradition from Virgil to Tennyson; yet all these conventions merge and float on the poet's marvelous symphonic word-music.

In the epilogue of the *Sequel*, "To the Leaven'd Soil They Trod," the poet treats simultaneously two themes: the return of the surviving soldiers to their homes after the soil of the nation has been "leavened" by the blood of the slain; and the effect of the war on Whitman's own poems:

> To the leaven'd soil they trod, calling, I sing, for the last;
>
>   . . . . .
>
> To the Alleghanian hills, and the tireless Mississippi,
> To the rocks I, calling, sing, and all the trees in
>   the woods,
> To the plain of the poems of heroes, to the prairie
>   spreading wide,

To the far-off sea, and the unseen winds, and the same
    impalpable air;
*. . . And responding, they answer all, (but not in words,)
The average earth, the witness of war and peace,
    acknowledges mutely;
The prairie draws me close, as the father, to bosom
    broad, the son;
The Northern ice and rain, that began me, nourish me
    to the end;
But the hot sun of the South is to ripen my songs.

Once again Walt Whitman is to be the poet of the whole
nation, now reconciled and united after the "leavening" of the
soil. Other Civil War poets (*e.g.*, Herman Melville in *Battle
Pieces*) sang this same theme of compassionate peace, but no
one better than Whitman in the two issues of *Drum-Taps*.

7

FOURTH EDITION (1867): When Whitman was finally able to
print a fourth edition of *Leaves of Grass*, again at his own
expense, it had to be a makeshift in order to reduce the cost.
The book was printed in New York on poor-quality paper, was
crudely bound, apparently in small batches as needed, and as a
consequence the surviving copies have many variations. Yet this
edition is important in the development of *Leaves of Grass*
because Whitman now began in earnest to revise and reassem-
ble his poems toward the ultimate shape of his final edition. He
used some of the plans and alterations he had begun in his
"Blue Book," but he failed to use so many of them that it
seems likely he had misplaced his annotated copy of the third

* Whitman's punctuation, not an editorial omission.

edition—or he may have simply changed his mind during the two-year interval.

This fourth edition opens with a new poem called "inscriptions," which in future editions would grow into a whole group of introductory poems with the title "Inscriptions." This poem summarizes the themes of *Leaves of Grass* as the poet now sees them:

> SMALL is the theme of the following Chant, yet the
> greatest—namely, ONE'S-SELF—that wondrous
> thing, a simple, separate person. That, for the
> use of the New World, I sing.
> Man's physiology complete, from top to toe, I sing.
> Not physiognomy alone, nor brain alone, is worthy
> for the muse;—I say the Form complete is worthier
> far. The female equally with the male, I sing.
> Nor cease at the theme of One's-Self. I speak the
> word of the modern, the word EN-MASSE.
> My Days I sing, and the Lands—with interstice I
> knew of hapless War.

> O friend, whoe'er you are, at last arriving hither
> to commence, I feel through every leaf the pressure
> of your hand, which I return. And thus upon our
> journey link'd together let us go.

After the announcement of this program, Whitman begins the book proper with the still further revised "Starting from Paumanok," followed by "Walt Whitman" (not yet "Song of Myself"). These two poems are the chants of "a simple, separate person . . . for the use of a New World." The second theme, "Man's physiology complete . . . female equally with the male," is, of course, the special subject of "Children of Adam" and "Calamus," and these follow "Walt Whitman." Beyond these groups, the six brief and unimportant new poems* and the remaining eighty-five from the previous editions are reshuffled according to some scheme which was emerging in the poet's mind but was not yet entirely clear. The earliest issue of this fourth edition ends with "Now Lift me Close" (a fragment of the 1860 "So Long!"), in which the poet imagines that the reader holding his book is in physical contact with him, as in the final verse of "Inscription." Later issues of the fourth edition (at least four issues are distinguishable) have *Drum-Taps*, the *Sequel*, and (in the fourth state) *Songs Before Parting*. Eventually Whitman would incorporate the war poems into *Leaves of Grass* as a "Drum-Taps" group, but in 1867 they are merely annexed, with original pagination and separate tables of contents.

In *Songs Before Parting* Whitman starts a new group though filled with old poems. The most important is "As I Sat Alone by Blue Ontario's Shore," a '56 poem based on passages fom the '55 Preface, adapted in '60 as "Chants Democratic" number 1, where it was "A Nation Announcing Itself . . ." The major theme in '67 is "the throes of Democracy," which shall make the nation stronger and finally invincible. For the '55–'56 call for "Bards" to lead democracy, the poet substitutes a vision-pageant in which a mother-figure commands him what to chant:

> As I sat alone, by blue Ontario's shore,
> As I mused of these mighty days, and of peace
>   return'd and the dead that return no more,
> A Phantom, gigantic, superb, with stern visage,
>   accost'd me;

* New: "Inscription" (later, "One's-Self I Sing"), "The Runner," "Tears! Tears!", "Aboard at Ship's Helm," "When I Read the Book," "The City Dead-House," "Leaflets, (What General)."

Chant me a poem, it said, *of the range of the high*
  Soul of Poets,
And chant of the welcome bards that breathe but my
  native air—invoke those bards;
And chant me, before you go, the Song of the throes
  of Democracy.

(Democracy—the destined conquer—yet treacherous lip-
  smiles everywhere,
And Death and infidelity at every step.)

The war has so intensified Whitman's nationalism that he
now insists that "nativity is answer enough to objections," success or failure depends entirely upon "ourselves." But the
danger within may be a susceptibility to alien, undemocratic
ideas:

America isolated I sing;
I say that works made here in the spirit of other
  lands, are so much poison to These States.

How dare these insects assume to write poems for America?
For our armies, and the offspring following the armies.

This mood of truculent nativism soon passed, and in the very
next edition of *Leaves of Grass* Whitman would cancel these
chauvinistic lines, but in 1867 the poet who "sat alone" by blue
Ontario spoke with a "barbed tongue," telling the nation not
what it wanted to hear but what he thought it needed to hear:
"Who are you, that wanted only a book to join you in your
nonsense?" Whitman's bardic conscience weighs so heavily
upon him that he must shout, prod, and bestir America to the
work still to be done. His conception of his duty is practically
the same as in 1855 (otherwise, such large segments of the '55
Preface could not be assimilated into this poem), but the
urgency is almost desperate.

In section 7 the poet sees another apparition "high toward heaven," which he calls "Libertad" (the Spirit of Liberty); she has returned "from the conqueress' field . . . with lambent lightning playing" around her head. Whether or not this is the same "Phantom" as in section 1, the personification is a similar armed mother-figure who now serves as Whitman's Americanized Muse. She sustains his courage and confidence (sec. 20):

> (Mother! bend down, bend close to me your face!
> I know not what these plots and deferments are for;
> I know not fruition's success—but I know that through
>   war and peace your work goes on, and must go on.)

Thus, "by blue Ontario's shore" the bard of "These States" closes his "chant" with an invocation to future "Bards for my own land . . ." The opening lines of "So Long!," the concluding poem of "Songs of Parting" and therefore of the fourth edition of *Leaves of Grass*, have not been changed since 1860, but they now have new significance:

> To conclude—I announce what comes after me,
> I announce mightier offspring, orators, days,
>   and then depart.

8

The theory of a *national* bard which Whitman first announced in his 1855 Preface had become almost an obsession with him in the years immediately following the Civil War. But whereas the ancient Welsh bards,[55] whose traditions certain British poets tried to revive in the eighteenth century, composed battle songs, celebrated military victories, and praised heroes, Whitman's bard was to be priest and moral leader. And he correctly observed that never had such leadership been more needed than in the first years of peace—Reconstruction or Gilded Age, as the corrupt period would later be called. In 1867–68 Whitman wrote two essays which he published in 1870 as a small book called *Democratic Vistas* to explain the role of the poet in the success or failure not only of the "American dream" but of humanity itself:

> View'd today, from a point of view sufficiently over-arching, the problem of humanity all over the civilized world is social and religious, and is to be finally met and treated by literature. The priest departs, the divine literatus comes. Never was anything more wanted than, today, and here in the States. . . . At all times, perhaps, the central point in any nation, and that whence it is itself really sway'd the most, and when it sways others, is its national literature, especially its archetypal poems. Above all previous lands, a great original literature is surely to become the justification and reliance (in some respects the sole reliance) of American democracy.[56]
>
> Few are aware how the great literature penetrates all, gives hue to all, all shapes aggregates and individuals, and, after subtle ways, with irresistible power, constructs, sustains, demolishes, at will. Why tower, in reminiscence, above all the nations of the earth, two special lands, petty in themselves, yet inexpressibly gigantic, beautiful, columnar? Immortal Judah lives, and Greece immortal lives, in a couple of poems.[57]

Parts of the 1855 Preface seem to rest on a theory of *representation*: the American poet must give expression to the social, moral, and political reality of his nation. But in 1856 ("The Eighteenth Presidency!") Whitman admitted how far the dream of an American democracy transcended the actuality, and in 1870 he found it just as remote:

Never was there, perhaps, more hollowness at heart than at present, and here in the United States. Genuine belief seems to have left us. The underlying principles of the States are not honestly believ'd in, (for all this hectic glow, and these melodramatic screamings), nor is humanity itself believ'd in. . . . We live in an atmosphere of hypocrisy . . . A scornful superciliousness rules in literature. . . . The depravity of the business classes of our country is not less than has been supposed, but infinitely greater. . . . I say that our New World democracy, however great a success in uplifting the masses out of their sloughs, in materialistic development, products, and in a certain highly deceptive superficial popular intellectuality, is, so far, an almost complete failure in its social aspects, and in really grand religious, moral, literary, and aesthetic results.[58]

Whitman's prose in *Democratic Vistas* is, as these quotations illustrate, wordy, ambiguous, and his syntax so loose that the reader must struggle to extract a coherent theory of poetry from it. What he seems to be saying is that poetry (or great literature) must provide models, archetypes, of personality, character, and modes of living capable of achieving the democratic society invisioned in the Declaration of Independence, the Constitution of the United States, and the Bill of Rights. He nowhere says this explicitly, but it seems to be the matrix for his repetitious condemnations of contemporary American literature, society, and government and his "vistas" of the correctives.

Central in Whitman's ideal male personality is pride in selfhood, a fierce spirit of independence, and emotional attachment to other men (Whitman's "Calamus" sentiment—more personal than the Christian concept of "brotherhood"). For women his ideal is "perfect mothers"—who scorn fashionable dress and frivolous social amusements, love children, feel equal to men, and are fond of an active, outdoor life. His women show no resemblance to contemporary heroines of fiction or drama, but they might have been found in the covered wagons on the Oregon trail. In fact, Whitman regarded the Western pioneers as archetypes of American democratic character; and so did he regard the average soldiers whom he had known during the war. While generals and politicians paltered and mismanaged, the soldiers sustained the poet's faith in human nature and gave him hope for the future of the country.

Democratic Vistas gives only glimpses of the society Whitman hoped to help create. Of course he takes for granted universal suffrage, even-handed justice, equal opportunity, etc. But "the mission of government is not repression . . . authority . . . not even law . . . but . . . to train communities through all grades, beginning with individuals and ending there again, to rule themselves." (He would certainly have approved of "community control" of schools.) "Of all dangers to a nation . . . there can be no greater than having certain portions of the people set off from the rest by a line drawn—they not privileged as others, but degraded, humiliated, made of no account."[59] He calls the "People" God's "divine aggregate," though if anyone insists on calling them, as some of his contemporaries did, the Devil's aggregate, Whitman still insists that they are "what democracy is for." A democratic society must be classless, not necessarily economically equal, but most citizens should be "middling property owners." Democracy needs "men and women with occupations, well-off, owners of houses and acres, and with cash in the bank—and with some craving for literature." No unemployed, or destitute, or ignorant.

Whitman has no political system to propose, because "Political democracy, as it exists and practically works in America, with all its threatening evils, supplies a training school for making first-class men. It is life's gymnasium, not of good only, but of all. We try often, though we fall back often." In the long run the effort and experience pay off, and literature can stimulate the effort and evaluate the experience. No more didactic conception of the nature and function of art has ever been proposed, though parallels could be found in the Renaissance theory of poetry, of Sir Philip Sidney, or Spenser—yet Whitman would have replied that they had used poetry to instruct princes and the elite: ". . . the great poems [of the past], Shakespeare included, are poisonous to the idea of the pride and dignity of the common people, the lifeblood of the democracy, the models of our literature as we get it from other lands, ultramarine, have had their birth in courts, and bask'd and grown in castle sunshine; all smells of princes' favor."

Yet in his moral and didactic theory of poetry Whitman was, in fact, more Renaissance than he knew, with the exception that *everyone* must be elite. As he had declared in "By Blue Ontario's Shore":

> Have you thought there could be but a single Supreme?
> There can be any number of Supremes—one does not
>   countervail another any more than one eyesight
>   countervails another, or one life countervails another.

When Whitman gets around to outlining "a basic model or portrait of personality for general use for the manliness of the State," he might almost be a Renaissance poet educating a prince for his duties, though the object of Whitman's instruction is princely only in owning no superior:

> To our model, a clear-blooded, strong-fibered physique is indispensable; the questions of food, drink, air, exercise, assimilation,

digestion, can never be intermitted. Out of these we descry a well-begotten selfhood—in youth, fresh, ardent, emotional, aspiring, full of adventure; at maturity, brave, perceptive, under control, neither too talkative nor too reticent, neither flippant nor somber; of the bodily figure, the movements easy, the complexion showing the best blood, somewhat flush'd, breast expanded, an erect attitude, a voice whose sound outvies music, eyes of calm and steady gaze, yet capable also of flashing—and a general presence that holds its own in the company of the highest.

Democratic Vistas contains one important pragmatic idea, that a democracy is not so much a political institution as a "training school" in character-formation—an experimental method for discovering how people can live together in a democratic manner. Yet, as a theory of the nature and function of poetry in a democratic society, it is pathetic; the boldly imaginative poet of the 1855 *Leaves of Grass* has so declined in creative imagination that he now outlines programs of hygiene and practical psychology to be taught by "model" personalities in his poems. And we are finally reminded of parallels with Stalinist Social Realism rather than of Renaissance guides for princes.

Whitman's poetic power had been receding since 1860, with a brief revival in the summer of 1865 while composing "When Lilacs Last in the Dooryard Bloom'd." By 1870 it had reached such a low ebb that the aging poet (only three years from crippling paralysis) had forgotten its source in his sensuous ecstasies two decades earlier, or his aching sexual longings of 1860. He is now retrospectively didacticizing (more accurate than D. H. Lawrence's "mentalizing") his poems and trying vainly to find some way of opening communication between himself and his abstraction "the People." Here we see him at his weakest. But no matter how desperately he might reshuffle his poems to teach his ideological "lessons," the great poems would remain masterpieces in world literature—in spite of some nicks and blemishes from the poet's endless revising. And he would yet be able occasionally to sublimate his old-age loneliness and spiritual hunger in poems of partly recovered lyrical power.

9

FIFTH EDITION (1872): The fifth edition of Leaves of Grass, like the fourth, is difficult to define. All issues bear the copyright date 1870, and the title page of the first issue reads 1871. It contains 384 pages, begins with "Inscriptions" (now increased to nine poems, though only two of them new), and contains the groups of the fourth edition (with variations in content) and some new ones. "Drum-Taps" for the first time becomes a group in the Leaves (261–98), and among the new groups are "Marches Now the War is Over," "Bathed in War's Perfume," and "Songs of Insurrection." But Whitman has removed about a third of the poems in the fourth edition, to start new collections that he would publish in 1871 as Passage to India (120 pages) and in 1872 as After All Not to Create Only and As a Strong Bird on Pinions Free.

In 1871 Whitman annexed Passage to India to Leaves of Grass, then in 1872 first As a Strong Bird and in a later issue the same year as After All. Thus the final issue of the fifth edition contains all the poems Whitman intended to include in Leaves of Grass, though he had not yet been able to assimilate the poems of the three pamphlets because of the piecemeal and improvised method of printing his book. None of the poems in these three pamphlets is of much importance except the title poem "Passage to India," but his preface to As a Strong Bird . . . (reprinted in 1881 in his Prose Works) shows that Leaves of Grass has reached a temporary climax.

Whitman's plan in 1872 was to terminate *Leaves of Grass* and to start a new collection, with "Passage to India" a key poem on death and immortality, probably to be called *Whispers of Heavenly Death*, though some of the poems in this group attached to *Passage to India* came from earlier editions. Whitman apparently felt that his early *Leaves* had not been sufficiently religious and spiritual. But the first paragraph of his Preface reveals his uncertainty and lack of confidence in his projected volume:

> The impetus and ideas urging me, for some years past, to an utterance, or attempt at utterance, of New World songs, and an epic of Democracy, having already had their published expression, as well as I can expect to give it, in *Leaves of Grass*, the present and any future pieces from me are really but the surplusage forming after that Volume, or the wake eddying behind it. I fulfilled in that an imperious conviction, and the commands of my nature as total and irresistible as those which make the sea flow, or the globe revolve. But of this Supplementary Volume, I confess I am not so certain. Having from early manhood abandoned the business pursuits and applications usual in my time and country, and obediently yielded myself up ever since to the impetus mentioned, and to the work of expressing those ideas, it may be that mere habit has got dominion of me, where there is no real need of saying anything further. . . .*60

Near the end of his Preface, Whitman shifts ground and tries to differentiate his two books:

> Leaves of Grass, already published, is, in its intentions, the song of a great composite *Democratic Individual*, male or female. And

---

* This is Whitman's punctuation at the end of this sentence, but the remaining half of the paragraph is omitted here, so the four periods serve a double purpose.

following on and amplifying the same purpose, I suppose I have in mind to run through the chants of this Volume, (if ever completed,) the thread-voice, more or less audible, of an aggregated, inseparable, unprecedented, vast, composite, electric *Democratic Nationality*.[61]

It is difficult to see how this distinction clarifies either Whitman's poetic ambitions or his projected division of his poems. Even in the 1855 edition he had seen his role both as giving expression to the pride of the individual in his selfhood and as influencing free men to build a freer society. And not least of the poet's functions ('55 Preface) was to "indicate [to men and women] the path between reality and their souls." Whitman's purposes had not shifted, nor had he acquired new subject matter. But in 1872 he felt a compelling urgency to *be more spiritual*. And he was not mindlessly repeating himself—or at least not entirely.

What had changed was not Whitman's ideas or his basic convictions but his emotions and the sources of his imaginative creations. In the 1855 "Song of Myself" he could find ecstasy —an almost auto-erotic pleasure—in his physiological sensations of respiration and inspiration, the beating of his heart, "the sniff of green leaves," the sound of his voice,

The feeling of health .... the full-noon trill . . .
    the song rising from bed and meeting the sun.

As stated in his first "inscription," "One's-Self I Sing," his theme in *Leaves of Grass* is "physiology from top to toe . . . Life immense in passion, pulse, and power . . ." But the second "inscription" for the fifth edition, "As I Ponder'd in Silence," indicates a shift in emphasis. A "Phantom . . . / The genius of

poets of old lands" reminds him that there is "but one theme
for ever-enduring bards . . . the theme of war, the fortune of
battles," and a Phantom asks what he sings. He replies that he,
too, sings war, though not the kind the epic poets of the past
sang, but

      —The field of the world;*
For life and death—for the Body, for the eternal Soul,
Lo! I too am come, chanting the chant of battles,
I, above all, promote brave soldiers.

The reader may be pardoned for being reminded of
"Onward, Christian Soldiers," for Whitman's battles are now
indeed moral ones, and his symbolical *phantoms, Souls,* and
communicating *birds* are closer to Christian allegory than to
the Lucretian naturalism of his earlier poems. Other symbols in
his poems have become more traditional too. A new group in
the "Passage to India" annex is called "Sea-Shore Memories,"
and these poems of 1860 (mainly) are mostly limited to sea-
shore subjects and imagery (a nesting mocking-bird on Long
Island, tides, sea-drift, the beach at night, etc.), but in "Passage
to India" the poet not only ventures out on "trackless seas,"
taking passage to India of "the Sanscrit and Vedas," but also,
anticipating his death, into "the seas of God."

In "Proud Music of the Storm" the poet and his Soul listen
to "a new rhythmus" for

Poems, bridging the way from Life to Death, vaguely
 wafted in night air, uncaught, unwritten,
Which, let us go forth in the full day, and write.

* *I.e.,* the world is the battlefield of Whitman's poems.

The *newness* of the rhythms are more imaginary than actual, but the spirit and the tone of these poems have changed from the *thought* of death in "Out of the Cradle" and "When Lilacs Last" to the *feeling* of its approach, which the poet's faith enables him to accept gladly in "Joy, Shipmate, Joy!," the closing poem in the "Passage to India" group:

> Joy! shipmate—joy!
> (Pleas'd to my Soul at death I cry;)
> Our life is closed—our life begins;
> The long, long anchorage we leave,
> The ship is clear at last—she leaps!
> She swiftly courses from the shore;
> Joy! shipmate—joy!

SIXTH EDITION (1876): Whitman's plan to make *Passage to India* the nucleus of a new volume of "chants of Death and Immortality" was thwarted by the poet's narrow escape, literally, from death early in 1873, when he suffered a stroke and partial paralysis. In 1876 he could only reprint the fifth edition of his *Leaves* as his Centennial edition in observance of the first century of the United States as a nation. But in a companion volume called *Two Rivulets* he offered a compromise substitute for a volume on Death and Immortality.

The title *Two Rivulets* has several meanings: first it is a companion volume to the Centennial issue of *Leaves of Grass*; second, it contains prose and poetry, with running footnote commentary, partly autobiographical, on the "Two Rivulets" section of poems—supplemented by *Democratic Vistas* and *Memoranda of the War*; and third, the "two rivulets" symbolize the poet and his reader "For the Eternal Ocean-bound." This conceit, ordinary in itself but given an original application, receives another twist of meaning in the next poem, "Or from that Sea of Time," which was not carried over into later editions of *Leaves of Grass*. The "sea of time" is not only the origin of life and its final receptacle (like Emerson's Over-Soul), but more specifically, the origin of the North American continent, the storms which have tested the durability of the American nation, and also the origin of Whitman's poems.

The key image for Whitman in 1876 is *shipwreck*, the result of his paralytic stroke, and he confessed to friends[62] that his "Prayer of Columbus" was his own prayer at that time:

> A batter'd wreck'd old man,
> Thrown on this savage shore, far, far from home,
> Pent by the sea, and dark rebellious brows, twelve
> dreary months,
> Sore, stiff with many toils, sicken'd and nigh to death,
> I take my way along the island's edge,
> Venting a heavy heart.
>
> I am too full of woe!
> Haply, I may not live another day;
> I can not rest, O God—I cannot eat nor drink nor sleep,
> Till I put forth* myself, my prayer, once more to Thee,
> Breathe, bathe myself once more in Thee—commune with Thee,
> Report myself once more to Thee.

Loss of his physical strength turned Whitman's thoughts more than ever to the unseen spiritual world which he believed to be the foundation of the visible world. In 1855 he had declared that the body and soul are one, but was disposed, as D. H. Lawrence observed, "to seize the soul by the scruff of her neck and plant her down among the potsherds," and tell her to

---

* Printed "forth forth," but the second "forth," evidently a typographical error, was deleted in 1881.

" 'Stay there! . . . Stay in the flesh, stay in the lips and in the belly, stay in the breast and womb. Stay there, O Soul, where you belong.' "[63] But this was the early Whitman, especially of the first edition of *Leaves of Grass*. It was not the Whitman of the later editions.

The Whitman of *Two Rivulets* believes in "Eidólons," the title of his third poem in the book, later transferred to "Inscriptions" in *Leaves of Grass*. He probably got the word, as W. S. Kennedy has surmised,[64] from P. G. Tait's *The Unseen Universe* (1875), which, in Kennedy's words, advances the hypothesis "that each organic or inorganic object on the earth makes, in the process of its growth, a delicate facsimile register of itself on the living sensitive ether that lies immediately around it and bathes and interpenetrates its every atom." The first six of the twenty-one stanzas give the substance of Whitman's poetic treatment of the idea:

I met a Seer,
Passing the hues and objects of the world,
The fields of art and learning, pleasure, sense, .
    To glean Eidólons.

Put in thy chants, said he,
No more the puzzling hour, nor day—nor segments, parts, put in,
Put first before the rest, as light for all, and entrance-
        song of all,
    That of Eidólons.

Ever the dim beginning;
Ever the growth, the rounding of the circle;
Ever the summit, and the merge at last, (to surely start again,)
    Eidólons! Eidólons!

Ever the mutable!
Ever materials, changing, crumbling, re-cohering;
Ever the ateliers, the factories divine,
   Issuing Eidólons!

Lo! I or you!
Or woman, man or State, known or unknown;
We seeming solid wealth, strength, beauty build,
   But really build Eidólons.

The ostent evanescent;
The substance of an artist's mood, or savan's studies long,
Or warrior's, martyr's, hero's toils,
   To fashion his Eidólons.

Whitman had always thought of himself as a duality of body and soul, but never before that his body was creating a soul around his body. Now, however, he finds pleasure in thinking that "the prophet and bard, / Shall yet maintain themselves—in higher stages yet . . ." and especially that his "Soul" will meet its "mates, Eidólons," that "the real I myself" is "an image, and Eidólon," and that even his poems create "A round, full-orb'd Eidólon."

10

SEVENTH EDITION (1881): Twenty-one years after the unlucky publication of the third edition of *Leaves of Grass* by Thayer and Eldridge, another Boston publisher, the highly respected James R. Osgood, brought out the seventh edition.[65] Whitman now had the opportunity to arrange his poems without worrying about printing costs and having to bind up unused printed sheets in such a hodgepodge as his last three editions.

Since 1876 he had written few poems of consequence, but he could now revise the contents of the groups he had already started and add new groups, filling them by shifting poems from positions which had not satisfied him. He did revise some lines and titles, but primarily the 1881 edition is important for fixing forever, so far as the poet was concerned, the order of his poems in *Leaves of Grass*. A threat of prosecution for obscenity soon caused Osgood to cease distribution and turn all rights, including the stereotype plates, over to Whitman,[66] who thereupon tried to become his own publisher again, but in a short time he turned the book over to a Philadelphia publisher, first to Rees Welsh and then to David McKay, who remained Whitman's publisher for the rest of his life. McKay reprinted *Leaves of Grass* several times, but always the 1881 edition, with two annexes in 1892 and thereafter.

In the 1881 *Leaves*, Whitman has increased his "Inscriptions" to twenty-four poems, and followed these "program" poems with the long "program" poem "Starting from Paumanok," succeeded in turn by "Song of Myself" (this title actually used for the first time in this edition). Then come "Children of Adam" and "Calamus." These "sex poems" are followed by twelve poems themselves arranged in a loose symbolical order which resembles the attempted allegorical form of the whole book, beginning with "Salut au Monde!," in which the poet explores his own inner (psychological) space, with variations on this theme in "Song of the Open Road" and "Crossing Brooklyn Ferry." This untitled group ends with "Youth, Day, Old Age, and Night"—the title suggesting the allegory alluded to above.

The third titled group is "Birds of Passage," a collection difficult to define but bound by a fragile thread-theme of the search of the human race for perfections ("Song of the Universal"), adventure ("Pioneers! O Pioneers!"), the French Revolution ("France"), each indebted to the past ("With Antecedents"). Immediately after this group comes "A Broadway Pageant," Whitman's vision of the migrations of civilization from Asia to Europe to America and back to Asia—this poem really does belong in "Birds of Passage." The poems in this group are not so much personal lyrics as moralizing odes, Whitman in his prophetic role.

Next in order comes "Sea-Drift," containing Whitman's great seashore lyrics ("Out of the Cradle Endlessly Rocking," and "As I Ebb'd with the Ocean of Life," etc.). Then comes another new group, "By the Roadside," a miscellany, beginning with the 1854 "A Boston Ballad" and ending with "To Identify the 16th, 17th or 18th Presidentiad" during the sleep-walking Gilded Age.

"Drum-Taps" now contains forty-three poems, and "Memories of President Lincoln" includes the four elegies on Lincoln. After an untitled group containing "Passage to India," "The Sleepers," and "To Think of Time," the remaining groups are "Autumn Rivulets," "Whispers of Heavenly Death," "From Noon to Starry Night," and "Songs of Parting," the latter ending with Whitman's now familiar epilogue "So Long!"

When these group titles are read in sequence, they sound grandly suggestive of the journey of a soul from its entrance into the world, with its *inscribed* portals, to its departure from physical existence. But usually the symbolical title is more appropriate for the key poem in the group than for the other poems. For all his care in selecting his group titles, and ceaseless revising and shifting of poems to find the best place for each, the order of the 1881 edition is still an improvisation. But it satisfied Whitman and he made it his *authorized* text. Future compositions would be added as "annexes" so as not to disturb this sacrosanct order.

Before McKay took over *Leaves of Grass*, Rees Welsh published a companion volume of Whitman's prose entitled *Specimen Days and Collect* (1882). "Specimen days" suggests a diary, and the most interesting portion of this division of the book is based on diary notes of the poet's experiences and observations during the Civil War, written, he explains in a footnote, in "blood-smutch'd little note-books" which he carried with him on his rounds in the hospitals and on the two occasions when he visited battlefields. No other writer of the period more vividly and convincingly described the feelings of the North after the defeat of the Union Army in the first battle at Bull Run and the fluctuating pulse of the nation through the uncertain years of the war.[67] Whitman also wrote unforgettable sketches of Lincoln during a pause in New York on his way to his first inauguration; and again as he rode through the capital on his way to the suburbs to escape the Washington heat; and still again on his second inauguration.[68] In these passages, and nearly all of *Specimen Days*, Whitman's prose is lucid, unaffected journalism so well written that it becomes literary art.

In *Specimen Days* Whitman was also taking a hand in his own biography. Just as he was striving so manfully to solidify his literary canon into an imperishable monument to himself, so also did he feel a compelling urge to begin shaping the biography of the poet of the *Leaves*, so that one would support the other. Dr. R. M. Bucke was writing a biography of Whitman, with the poet's help, and in 1881 they visited together the homesteads and cemeteries of the Whitmans and Van Velsors on Long Island.[69] Supplied with fresh memories and reminders of his origin, Whitman set about interpreting his early life and the three centuries of his family history. These he used to introduce "Specimen Days." The nature notes which he wrote outdoors at Timber Creek during his recuperation in the late 1870s made an effective close.

To fill out the book, Whitman added "Democratic Vistas" and a "Collect" of his prefaces and literary essays, and at the very end a selection of "Pieces in Early Youth." He confessed that these juvenile poems and short stories had little literary value, but their inclusion is another reminder that the old poet wanted to put all the documents of his literary career on record, to be available to future students of his life and works.

In 1888 Whitman published a thin volume of poetry and prose which he called *November Boughs*. For preface and a summing up of his whole career he reprinted a long essay called "A Backward Glance O'er Travel'd Roads."[70] He now wanted *Leaves of Grass* to be judged not as literature, in which he feared it was deficient, but as a "personal record . . . an attempt to put *a Person*, a human being (myself, in the latter half of the Nineteenth Century, in America,) freely, fully and truly on record."

"Sands at Seventy" includes the poems, mostly brief lyrics and epigrams of an old man acutely aware of his mortality, which Whitman had written since the printing of the 1881 edition of his *Leaves*. But he had not yet reached the end of his "travel'd road." In 1891 he published a still thinner volume of poems and prose entitled *Good-Bye My Fancy*. The prose consists of more miscellaneous literary essays, none of distinction. The poems begin with "Sail out for Good, Eidólon Yacht!"

Depart, depart for solid earth—no more returning
  to these shores,
          .   .   .   .   .
Sail out for good, eidólon yacht of me!

and ends with the title poem "Good-Bye My Fancy!" The poet
and his fancy will "die together, (yes, we'll remain one,) . . .
Good-bye and hail! My Fancy." Did ever a poet prepare more
assiduously to die? He wanted his demise to be symbolical, too,
and to nourish the mythology of his *Leaves of Grass*, which he
confidently expected to live for centuries.

EIGHTH EDITION (1888): This is primarily of interest to collec-
tors. After publishing *November Boughs*, Whitman combined
his 1881 *Leaves of Grass*, his *Specimen Days and Collect*, and
November Boughs in one huge volume which he called *Complete Poems and Prose*. He used the stereotype plates of three
separate books, with their original pagination, without corrections.

NINTH EDITION (1892): The 1892 edition of *Leaves of Grass*
(copyrighted 1891 but with 1892 on the title page) is mainly a
reprint of the 1881 text plus the two annexes, "Sands at Seventy" and "Good-Bye My Fancy," prefaced by "An Executor's
Diary Note, 1891," placing upon his executor "the injunction
that whatever may be added to the *Leaves* shall be supplementary . . . " In other words, he wants all future editions to be
based on this text, with any unpublished poems added as further annexes. In 1897, Whitman's executors did publish a tenth
edition of the *Leaves*, with thirteen uncollected poems in a
third annex called "Old Age Echoes," thus piously carrying out
his commands.

The 1892 *Leaves of Grass* has become known as Whitman's
"Deathbed Edition," and has consistently been reprinted with
this claim. Whitman's true deathbed edition was a very limited
and private one, of about one hundred copies.[71] In the autumn
of 1891 his closest friends in Camden and Philadelphia thought
he would not live to see bound copies of his ninth edition, then
in process of being printed from a text which he had himself

prepared with the help of Horace Traubel, who acted as his errand boy and proofreader. This final text was still mainly the 1881 edition, plus the two annexes, though Whitman made a few corrections.

In order that the old poet might hold a copy of a new edition of his poems in his hands while he was still conscious, Traubel, with the help of the printers, who were also devoted to Whitman, hastily assembled from printed sheets left over from the late issues of the *Leaves* a special issue just for the poet and ten or twelve of his most intimate friends. This book Whitman did have the pleasure of handling some time in November, though he was too ill to read it; and he presented copies as Christmas presents to his devoted circle. Though today a very rare collector's item, this deathbed edition is not the true authorized text of 1892, on which Harold Blodgett and Sculley Bradley have based their "Comprehensive Reader's Edition" of *Leaves of Grass* (1965) in the definitive *Collected Writings of Walt Whitman*.[72]

There can be no doubt that the 1892 text is the one Whitman wanted the world to remember and cherish, and it is the most complete edition personally supervised and approved by him. But as for the twelve poems originally published in 1855, the text of the first edition is more imaginative, more spontaneous, more vital. For the "Calamus" and "Children of Adam" poems and "Out of the Cradle Endlessly Rocking" (though called "A Word Out of the Sea" in 1860), the text of the third edition is recommended; moreover, the third edition (reprinted in 1961) is the only edition which has true unity and really significant order.

After 1860 the first book publication of a poem is less important, and the final text is nearly as good as any other—and often more polished. Of the first seven editions, none has such power as the first and third; thus, the reader might as well settle for the "authorized" text of 1892 or the "Comprehensive Reader's Edition" (1965), augmented by all the uncollected poems and poem fragments which have survived in manuscripts. From first to last, therefore, *Leaves of Grass* is not so much one book as a series of anthologies containing, in flux, all of Walt Whitman's poems (except the juvenile verse), which he ceaselessly revised, pruned, and augmented between 1855 and 1892.

IV ROOT-CENTER

There is . . . in the make-up of every superior human identity
. . . a soul-sight of that divine clue and unseen thread which
holds the whole congeries of things . . . root-center for the mind.
                    —"Carlyle from an American Point of View"

1

Though there are a number of books (see Chapter III) called
Leaves of Grass, the public will doubtless continue to think of
the 1891–92 text (in whatever modern edition) as *Leaves of
Grass*. For practical purposes, then, let us think of this book as
a single literary work without regard to the chronology of the
separate poems, and see what it is, what central themes or subject matter gives it unity, if any. Some critics have tried to
interpret it as an American epic,[1] others as a collection of personal lyrics (the longer ones perhaps some variety of "ode"),[2]
and an admiring few as a "Bible of Democracy."[3] Though only
a small group of "disciples" (the poet's most intimate friends
during his last years) have gone so far as to regard *Leaves of
Grass* as sacred scripture, it is nevertheless true that Whitman
is best known throughout the world as the "Poet of Democracy." There must be reasons why this book is so difficult to
classify.

The breakdown of literary genres began in the early years of the European Romantic movement, but it was accentuated in American literature by the literary development which came to be known as American Transcendentalism, of which Ralph Waldo Emerson was the chief spokesman or protagonist during the gestation of Whitman's *Leaves*. As has often been observed by literary historians, within the space of five years the majority of the great masterpieces of nineteenth-century American literature were published: Hawthorne's *Scarlet Letter* in 1850, Melville's *Moby Dick* in 1851, Thoreau's *Walden* in 1854, and *Leaves of Grass* in 1855. Of these authors, only Thoreau was closely associated with the Transcendentalist group; but they all made extensive use of symbols—in language, literary structure, and themes—which originated in or were influenced by the Transcendentalist theories, even Hawthorne and Melville, though they scorned the movement.

Basically, these authors used images of physical things as metaphors or symbols of mental experiences, which they believed to be somehow intimately related to an unseen spiritual source. More concisely: the external world of "nature" reflected an invisible inner reality. Emerson believed that man's obvious defects and weaknesses were the result of his having become alienated from "nature"; this separation was Emerson's substitute for "original sin," which he vehemently rejected. If this breach between man and nature could be healed, he might become a Godlike creature and build a Paradise on earth. Man could recover this harmony by listening to the voice of his conscience and following the intuitions of the Soul, both his own and the universal Over-Soul.

"Nature always wears the colors of spirit," Emerson declared in his essay "Nature." And again: "This relation between the mind and matter is not fancied by some poet, but stands in the will of God, and so is free to be known by all men. . . . Man is conscious of a universal soul within or behind his individual life, wherein, as in a firmament, the nature of Justice, Truth, Love, Freedom, arise and shine. This universal soul he calls Reason: it is not mine, or thine, or his, but we are its; we are its property and men."[4] As a consequence, "It is not words only that are emblematic; it is things which are emblematic. Every natural fact is a symbol of some spiritual Truth. Every appearance corresponds to some state of the mind, and that state of the mind can be described by presenting that natural appearance as its picture."[5]

Writers who viewed their world in this symbolical way wanted to work like Nature herself, composing not by conscious design within traditional patterns, but letting their literary work grow organically like leaves and fruit on a tree, nourished by some miraculous spiritual energy. To avoid unintelligible disorder and incoherence, these writers usually employed a journey motif or a symbolical time sequence. Thoreau used both in his first book, *A Week on the Concord and Merrimack Rivers*. But even so, the *Week* is a miscellany; the journey is mainly the sequence of thoughts, memories, fantasies which Thoreau recorded in his notebooks not only during the actual boat trip with his brother on the two rivers but also during the ten years following the trip, before he finally completed his manuscript. The journey is, therefore, psychological. *Walden* is less of a miscellany, but it is also held together by a symbolical structure based on the seasons in the locale of Walden Pond. In language and style it is more poetical (*i.e.*, metaphysical in language and lyrical in emotional tone) than Thoreau's poems, which are stiff, awkward, and labored, because the conventional prosodic forms restricted the spontaneous flow of his thought and expression. Emerson's most successful literary form was the essay. He had difficulty in organizing his ideas even in this loose genre, but it gave his imagination the freedom it needed to select metaphors at will and to expand or contract them as his feeling dictated.

Melville, the anti-Transcendentalist, intent on piercing the wall separating physical reality and whatever lies behind it, giving it existence—and he had strong suspicions that nothing did—was a Transcendentalist in practice, depending upon symbols to explore the origin and meaning of experience. In *Moby Dick* he, too, achieved a measure of coherence by a journey motif, but the literary work defies classification. Looked at in one way, it is an epic; in another way, a tragic drama. It is not a novel, almost a poem; it combines features of almost every literary genre, yet violates and transcends all genres.

Leaves of Grass is also such a genre-defying work, a Transcendental miscellany, as individual as Thoreau's *Week* or an Emerson essay, with its own free-flowing structure. Viewed as a whole (in the final version), it is part autobiography, part lyric, part sermon or sociological tract. The great dilemma, in fact, when it is examined aesthetically and logically, is how to reconcile the *mélange* (one of Whitman's favorite words) of lyricism and socio-political didacticism. Having composed conventional (though mediocre) verse in his earlier writing career, Whitman knew what the conventions were. But in writing *Leaves of Grass* he, like Thoreau and Melville, was attempting to create something unknown in the history of literary genres and conventions. When in "A Backward Glance O'er Travel'd Roads" (1888), Whitman warned that "No one will get at my verses who insists upon viewing them as a literary performance, or attempt at such performance, or as aiming mainly toward art or aestheticism,"[6] he was not simply making excuses for his failures, admitting finally that he was not a poet but something else. He believed firmly that the time had come for "a readjustment of the whole theory and nature of poetry." Actually he had believed this as early as 1855, when he wrote his famous 1855 Preface. But now he urged a "readjustment," after nearly thirty-five years of experience in making his own adjustment.

The fact, however, that Whitman continued over so many years to write prefaces and reminiscent essays on his purposes in *Leaves of Grass* is a strong indication that he was never entirely sure himself what had motivated him in composing his poems, or even what his purposes were. In "A Backward Glance" he confessed: "After completing my poems, I am curious to review them in the light of their own (at the time unconscious, or mostly unconscious) intentions, with certain unfoldings of the thirty years they seek to embody."[7] This confession is useful in examining *Leaves of Grass* by the theories he announced at various stages of the unfolding of his *Leaves*, each time professing the conscious intentions which he was willfully trying to achieve.

Even though Whitman did not know what restless inner urge caused him to seek relief—or satisfaction—in composing poems, later he rationalized his creative activity with theories of his "intentions" and the "meanings" of his poems. While he was seeing his third edition through the press in Boston, a friend asked him how his "first poems impressed him, at this re-reading," and he replied: "I am astonished to find myself capable of feeling so much."[8] One can only guess which of his "first poems" now seemed to him to have such astonishing "feeling," but certainly one was "Song of Myself" (still in 1860 called "Walt Whitman"). But naming the specific titles he had in mind is less important than the fact that the intensity of emotion experienced in composing some of the earlier poems—and incorporated and retained in them—was transitory, as every emotional experience must be. During the creative act the poet *feels* his thoughts and images; afterwards he remembers them symbolically, thinks about them perhaps and cerebrates theories, explanations, rationalizations.

Malcolm Cowley's deduction[9] that Whitman wrote his 1855 Preface after he had completed the twelve poems—after his exhilaration had subsided and he had begun to *misunderstand* his creation—fits the above hypothesis. Cowley suggests that a mystical experience enabled Whitman to write "Song of Myself" and two or three other poems in the first edition; furthermore, that the sense of power which the experience gave him, and which he did not understand, made him arrogant afterwards. This theory is at least partly suggested by the fact that the 1855 Preface, and the self-written reviews that Whitman published anonymously soon after the publication of this book, do not seem to have come from the same mind and personality.[10]

The author says at the beginning of his first poem in the first edition that he celebrates himself only as an example of the selfhood available to all men. Moreover, the "Song of Myself" is concerned above all else with the relation of body and soul and the physical and spiritual worlds. Though permeated by the imagery of American life, the emphasis in the poem is not on *American* but on *life*; or rather on birth, life, and death, for the major motif is the eternal cycle of existence in both the cosmic and the spiritual realms. The 1855 Preface, however, describes "a bard [who] is to be commensurate with a people," and especially the citizens of the United States. This bard will lead the American people in matching the size, abundance, fecundity, and beauty of the North American continent by an unprecedented development of their own several characters. The Preface is nationalistic through and through, but on a highly idealistic plane. One can see a difference between the poet of "Song of Myself" and the author of the Preface, but the difference is not irreconcilable.

However, when Whitman began to write anonymous reviews of his book, he turned chauvinistic with a vengeance. His self-written review for the almost frenetically nationalistic *United States Review* was quoted in Chapter III,[11] wherein Whitman saluted "an American bard at last!" and enumerated what he regarded as his own claims to the title. But his review for the Brooklyn *Times* placed even more emphasis on the poet who had exhibited in his poems "his own flesh and form, undraped," without modesty and with great pride in being "a rude child of the people!" This was the beginning of the holy barbarian author of *Leaves of Grass*.

These two Whitmans, the ontological poet of such masterpieces as "Song of Myself" and the nationalistic spokesman in the prefaces and reviews (an idealist in most of the prefaces but a jingoist and exhibitionist in the anonymous reviews), can be seen in all parts of the final *Leaves of Grass*. Sometimes he is both in the same poem, but more often he is either using language aesthetically (as in the major poems, such as "Song of Myself," "The Sleepers," "Out of the Cradle . . . ," "When Lilacs Last . . . ," etc.) or he is proclaiming a program. The point is that Whitman did not see the difference, because, as he said, he did not aim at "Art or aestheticism," and the poems were written out of "unconscious, or mostly unconscious," intentions, while the programs to explain the poems were very consciously—even self-consciously—contrived.

2

To analyze *Leaves of Grass* separately as lyric, epic, or doctrine, one must dissect and, to an extent, mutilate the poems. One of these elements may be found to be more prominent in this poem or that, but no poem is all lyric or all epic, though a few come close to being all doctrine. The book opens with "One's-Self I Sing," which was quoted in Chapter III in the version from the fourth edition; this is the final version:

One's-Self I sing, a simple separate person,
Yet utter the word Democratic, the word En-Masse.

Of physiology from top to toe I sing,
Not physiognomy alone nor brain alone is worthy for
   the Muse, I say the Form complete is worthier far,
The Female equally with the Male I sing.

Of Life immense in passion, pulse, and power,
Cheerful, for freest action form'd under the laws divine,
The Modern Man I sing.

This poem is nearly all doctrine, announcing the "program" of the book. Except for slightly inverted syntax and a smattering of alliteration (such as the s sound in line 1 and the p in line 7), the lines read almost like prose—though nearer the prose of oratory than the prose of the daily newspaper. The two most prominent characteristics of a lyric, musicality and subjectivity, are not prominent in this poem. The poet says "I sing," but here *sing* is a metaphor, not a fact. Since the poem is not singable, why does the poet use the word *sing* four times? Probably because he remembered that the epic poet sang—Homer quite literally—according to tradition. And Virgil begins his epic, "Arms and the man I sing." In defending his subject matter as "worthy for the Muse," Whitman is asserting that his muse is different from Homer's or Virgil's because he sings for a democratic society. Consequently, his hero is not a giant among men, a Hector or an Achilles, but "a simple separate person"—an average person, but one with his own personality.

Separate but not isolated—there are no Captain Ahabs in *Leaves of Grass*.

The second *Inscription*, "As I Ponder'd in Silence," continues the poet's defense of his kind of singing. The Phantom spirit of "poets of old lands" reminds him that "there is but one theme for ever-enduring bards . . . the theme of War, the fortune of battles, / The making of perfect soldiers." Whitman replies that he also sings of war and heroism, but his battlefield is the world and his soldiers are fighting the battle of life and death. This program is so broad that it might be for any age or society. But it is *moral*, and promoting moral character is Whitman's deepest conscious purpose in *Leaves of Grass*.

In another *Inscription*, "I Hear America Singing," the song of each American is his or her life-contribution as workman, mother, wife, a human identity. The thought is also a didactic cliché, but in his roll call of the different workers Whitman does achieve a lyricism which has enabled several musicians to set the poem successfully to music—notably Harvey Gaul, George Kleinsinger, and Norman Lockwood.

Another means by which Whitman makes his subjectivity lyrical is the game he plays with his reader, as in the two-line *Inscription* "To you!":

> Stranger, if you passing meet me and desire to speak
>   to me, why should you not speak to me?
> And why should I not speak to you?

Here, without a doubt, the man is speaking as well as the poet, for Whitman admitted in his preface to *Two Rivulets* that he had written his poems out of loneliness, "to arouse and set flowing in men's and women's hearts, young and old (my present and future readers) endless streams of living, pulsating love and friendship directly from them to myself, now and ever."[12] Whitman's poems are at least personal in this desire—always latent and frequently expressed—to establish an intimacy with his reader, whom he often addressed as "you" or "you up there"; that is, the reader holding the book. In a "Backward Glance" he defines the ego in his poems as "the one chanting or talking, toward himself and toward his fellow-humanity."[13] It would seem to be significant that he does not say the ego is his own, but uses the indefinite *one*. The Jung-oriented critic would say a *persona*, which is neither entirely fictional nor symbolical. At times the "one" speaking is Walt Whitman the man; at other times, a symbolical "I" which is Whitman's ego magnified and idealized—a fantasy personality.

The way the real and the symbolical "I" can merge is demonstrated in "Starting from Paumanok." Walt Whitman did start life on "fish-shape Paumanok," and he always seemed to think his mother "perfect," as the poem states. He had also dwelt in Manhattan and for a few weeks in New Orleans. But beyond these simple facts, the "I" of the poem becomes fabulous: a soldier, a miner in California, a woodsman in Dakota—almost a personification of the pioneers who were taking possession of the vast continent and making it into a nation.

Space, too, is symbolical in *Leaves of Grass*. In section 2 the poet envisions the revolving globe waiting and preparing for the democratic society he is prophesying:

See, vast trackless spaces,
As in a dream they change, they swiftly fill,
Countless masses debouch upon them,
They are now cover'd with the foremost people, arts,
    institutions known.

See, projected through time,
For me an audience interminable.

With firm and regular step they wend, they never stop,
Successions of men, Americanos a hundred millions,
One generation playing its part and passing on,
Another generation playing its part and passing on in its turn,
With faces turn'd sideways or backward toward me to listen,
With eyes retrospective toward me.

In this prophetic role he will (sec. 6) "trail the whole geography of the globe and salute courteously every city large and small"—obviously a flight of the imagination, though for a number of years Whitman did entertain the ambition to become a wandering poet-lecturer,[14] an apostle of his democratic religion, which he did not confine to his own country. He expects to find heroism in the lives of all the people he meets "upon land and sea," but "will report all heroism from an American point of view."

In section 7 this poet declares:

I am the credulous man of qualities, ages, races,
I advance from the people in their own spirit,
Here is what sings unrestricted faith.

The faith is not only in the "heroism" innate in human nature, but also, and because of, the faith that every particle of the universe "has reference to the soul" (sec. 12). This program for *Leaves of Grass* rests firmly on Emerson's doctrine of "correspondences" mentioned above:

Melange mine own, the unseen and the seen,
Mysterious ocean where the streams empty,
Prophetic spirit of materials shifting and flickering
    around me . . .

Whitman's *mélange* is, therefore, not simply a homogenized equality of every finite being, but also a commingling of the finite and the infinite. No one can hold a more democratic philosophy than that. But it is just such a doctrine which affords Whitman his wealth of double metaphors, enabling him to utilize the objects, geography, space, etc., of the physical world to express subjective states of mind and emotions. And nearly all the objects mentioned in "Starting from Paumanok" reappear in other poems in *Leaves of Grass*, some becoming expanded metaphors or symbols, such as the mockingbird in Alabama (sec. 11) and the mockingbird *from* Alabama on Long Island in "Out of the Cradle . . ." Physical space (sec. 6) becomes the inner space of "Salut au Monde!": "What widens within you, Walt Whitman?"

But the most important use Whitman makes of his double metaphor is to strengthen his prophetic vision, to translate his abstractions into concrete images, and vice versa, as in section 17:

Expanding and swift, henceforth,
Elements, breeds, adjustments, turbulent, quick and audacious,
A world primal again, vistas of glory incessant and branching,
A new race dominating previous ones and grander far, with new
    contests,
New politics, new literatures and religions, new inventions
    and arts.

These, my voice announcing—I will sleep no more but arise,
You oceans that have been calm within me! how I feel you,
    fathomless, stirring, preparing unprecedented waves
    and storms.

This passage is an excellent illustration of Whitman animating his dogmas. It begins dynamically: "Expanding and swift . . . ," then the enumeration of the abstractions, followed by "A world primal again, vistas of glory incessant and branching." This is logically ambiguous, but "primal" suggests the Garden of Eden, the sight of distant and future landscapes, and the continuity of "glory incessant and branching" visual empathy.[15] Then the "ocean" the poet feels stirring within himself, so completely has he identified his feelings with his prophecy, becomes apocalyptic—almost an allegory on several levels of metaphorical associations of images.

When Whitman fails to make the translation of his abstractions into sensory images, as he fails to do in a number of the *Inscription* poems, the composition remains more "program" than poem—though sometimes by vehemence of assertion he can charge his dry utterances with emotion. Curiously, Whitman frequently seems not to be writing poems but announcing what he is going to put in his poems, and yet he often does make a poem out of his program for poems, as in "Starting from Paumanok."

3

Near the end of his life Whitman, as we have noticed, liked to think of his completed *Leaves of Grass* as "a poem" which had taken him a lifetime to write. But his last edition was *a poem* only in his private sense of the term. In his 1855 Preface he had called the United States a poem, and after stating his creed had given the command to "read these leaves in the open air every season of your life, re-examine all you have been told at school or church or in any book, dismiss whatever insults your own soul, and your very flesh shall be a great poem and have the richest fluency not only in its words but in the silent lines of its lips and face and between the lashes of your eyes and in every motion and joint of your body."[16] But this is only a figurative way of saying that the reader may become the incarnated "poem"—the poem made flesh—Whitman was trying to write.

The book of *Leaves of Grass* is not one poem in any common denotation of the word, but the whole book can be said to be permeated with lyric emotion, for the poems are predominantly imaginative, subjective, emotional, and symbolical. In many of the "program poems" the statement (prose element) adulterates the lyricism, but even in these the world is a dream (fantasy) world, and the godlike *persona* has miraculous powers to lead, heal, transcend time and space, and project a new Garden of Eden. Even in the finest lyrics, didacticism is not entirely absent, but it is submerged and suffused by feeling rather than teaching.

Almost every critic will agree that "Song of Myself" is Whitman's supreme lyric. He would deserve the rank of major poet if he had written nothing else. It has been remarked that all Western philosophy is only footnotes to Plato, and one might say in the same hyperbole that the remainder of *Leaves of Grass* consists of footnotes to "Song of Myself." But this is a half-truth, like the epigram on Western philosophy. It can be said, however, that in "Song of Myself" Whitman almost exhausted—in the sense both of completion and of depletion—his greatest lyrical impulse.

What was that lyrical impulse? It was more than the poet's desire to "sing himself," or to "put his life on record." That "Song of Myself" is about the realization of the meaning of *self* or *selfhood*, nearly all critics agree.[17] But why should this realization give the poet the ecstasy which suffuses the poem and endows the *persona* with lyrical power of expression? A pat explanation is that Whitman had undergone what William

James in his *Varieties of Religious Experience* calls "a mystical experience." In fact, James cites section 5 of "Song of Myself" as "a classical expression of this sporadic type of mystical experience." [18] He quotes only half of this passage, but since it is a key to Whitman's lyricism, the whole section deserves quotation:

> I believe in you my soul, the other I am must not
>   abase itself to you,
> And you must not be abased to the other.
>
> Loafe with me on the grass, loose the stop from your throat,
> Not words, not music or rhyme I want, not custom or lecture,
>   not even the best,
> Only the lull I like, the hum of your valvèd voice.
>
> I mind how once we lay such a transparent summer morning,
> How you settled your head athwart my hips and gently turn'd
>   over upon me,
> And parted the shirt from my bosom-bone, and plunged your
>   tongue to my bare-stript heart,
> And reach'd till you felt my beard, and reach'd till you
>   held my feet.
>
> Swiftly arose and spread around me the peace and knowledge
>   that pass all the arguments of the earth,
> And I know that the hand of God is the promise of my own,
> And I know that the spirit of God is the brother of my own,
> And that all the men ever born are also my brothers, and
>   the women my sisters and lovers,
> And that a kelson of the creation is love,
> And limitless are leaves stiff or drooping in the fields,
> And brown ants in the little wells beneath them,
> And mossy scabs of the worm fence, heap'd stones, elder,
>   mullein and poke-weed.

James found that experiences of this kind, during which the protagonist feels a sense of union with some mysterious presence or in-flowing energy, often similar to the exhilaration and climax of sexual intercourse, were very common in the history of "religious experiences," thousands of which have been preserved in the literature of the subject. James admitted that such experiences often seem to be pathological, but he was unwilling to say whether they were actually the result of a union of a finite consciousness with an infinite one or were delusional—an aberration of the nervous system. In either case, James insisted, the experience was *real* to the mind experiencing it. As a psychologist, he could discover the conditions which created a favorable environment for these experiences, such as prayer, fasting, penitence, worship of a deity or spirit, etc.; he could examine the after-effects, which almost invariably included a sense of brotherhood, an acute appreciation of the beauty and equality of everything that exists, and a conviction that love animates all creation—Whitman's "kelson." Usually, also, the subject seems to feel *his self* being absorbed into a larger or universal *Self*. Paradoxically, the self shrinks to nothing at the same time it becomes omnipotent in its union with a Higher Self. All these results are enumerated in Whitman's union of body and soul, though the self-abnegation of some Eastern mystics is absent; his self becomes so confident as to seem arrogant. Like the mystics of nearly all lands and times, however, he, too, believed (see Chapter II) that "The ignorant man is demented with the madness of owning things . . . ," a belief which turned him from business pursuits to the unprofitable occupation of full-time poet.

James thought the experience described in section 5 was probably sporadic, and in a footnote he remarks that "Whitman in another place [*Specimen Days*] expresses in a quieter

way what was probably with him a chronic mystical perception":

"There is," he says, "apart from mere intellect, in the make-up
of every superior human identity, a wondrous something that
realizes without argument, frequently without what is called education (though I think it the goal and apex of all education
deserving the name), an intuition of the absolute balance, in
time and space, of the whole of this multifariousness we call *the
world*; a soul-sight of that divine clue and unseen thread which
holds the whole congeries of things, all history and time, and all
events, however trivial, however momentous, like a leashed dog
in the hand of a hunter. [Of] such soul-sight and root-centre for
the mind mere optimism explains only the surface."[19]

This kind of "perception" is indeed the "root-centre" of
Leaves of Grass, as almost any page will show, and Whitman
says that "every superior human identity" has it. Of course,
"superior" qualifies its prevalence, but he implies that by cultivating this "intuition" a person may attain a "superior human
identity." But whether Whitman himself was a "sporadic" or a
"chronic" mystic by James's definitions is less important than
the use he makes in *Leaves of Grass* of his "mystic perception."
As pointed out in Chapter II, in his preparatory notes he was
fascinated by the idea that "The effusion or corporation of the
soul is always under the beautiful laws of physiology."[20] In section 5 of "Song of Myself" he dramatizes—to some extent
mythologizes—such an "effusion." He was always, he says, conscious of himself as two, "my soul and I"—two levels of consciousness, the modern psychologist would say.

The union of the poet's soul and body could have been a
myth of his creative imagination rather than a true reminiscence, but if so either it was so powerful a myth that it ener-

gized his own mind and body or it served as symbol of the radiant happiness which he had already attained in the harmony of his faith and sensibility. "Song of Myself" is a lovely song of praise for all created things, from men to ants and common weeds in the field, because the poet feels so strongly "the spirit of God" (love) to be "the brother" of his own. In this sense Whitman is pre-eminently a religious poet.

One aspect, at least, of Whitman's poetic description of the union of his soul and body was genuinely experienced, and accurately symbolized as a sexual union, whatever variety of mysticism we may call it. Whitman knew that religious emotion and sexual hunger had common origins in his psyche. Traubel reports his remarking to Thomas Harned: "I think Swedenborg was right when he said there was a close connection—a very close connection—between the state we call religious ecstasy and the desire to copulate. I find Swedenborg confirmed in all my experience."[21] It is significant that Whitman does not equate religious ecstasy with sexual orgasm but with *sexual desire*. Of course, the orgasm brings relief from the tension of desire, and if the satisfaction is only in fantasy, then the expression (in words) of the fantasy is the poet's means of relieving the tension. Thus the permeating sexuality in Whitman's poems had both a personal and an intellectual-aesthetic function, and was in the broadest sense a union of his body and mind, resulting in psychological therapy and sociological program.

Edwin H. Miller in his *Walt Whitman's Poetry: a Psychological Journey* is explicitly Freudian in his comments on section 5, which he calls the record of Whitman's "epiphany":

The scene is a startling, audacious portrait of an artist who has retreated from the artificialities of society to contemplate a "spear of summer grass." Alone, nude, searching for a "reality" that is true to the self, not a cultural imposition upon the self, he opens his atrophied senses to the natural rhythms of the universe. No longer is his body checked in its natural desire for tactile sensation, his ears hear "the belched words of my voice," and his nose greedily absorbs the "perfumes" of the woods. For with his clothes he has shed value judgments and guilt in order to "possess the origin of all poems." Freed from chronological time and from sexual fears and inhibitions, he is ready for the regressive journey to the depths of his being.[22]

By "regressive journey" this psychoanalytical critic means that Whitman in his fantasy has returned to the submerged images and desires of his childhood, a time when he found satisfaction in oral and tactile contacts with his mother. "The source of his impact upon his readers, at least those who do not protect themselves by normalizing Whitman, is that he taps subterranean currents that we have tried to forget when we put away childish things. Human beings hunger for the oral and tactile gratifications which Whitman candidly acknowledges." Thus making himself in imagination a child again, he emancipated himself from the unhealthy restrictions of his repressive society: ". . . Whitman resurrects the body . . . makes the soul sensual once again . . ."[23] By so doing, Whitman also became an artist, a poet, whose role was to be the liberation of others in the process of achieving his own liberation.

4

Through his epiphany, Whitman likewise learned two of his most important poetic techniques, those of *identification* and *vision*. To consider identification first: Whitman many times uses the word *identity* (cf. "human identity" in James's quota-

tion above from *Specimen Days*) both in prose and in poetry
to signify the yoking of soul and body at the birth of a human
being; in other words, to attain "identity" is to take one's place
in the endless procession of souls on the road to *selfhood*,
which, once attained, is indestructible. For example, in "To
Think of Time" (sec. 7):

> It is not to diffuse you that you were born of your mother
>   and father, it is to identify you,
> It is not that you should be undecided, but that you should
>   be decided,
> Something long preparing and formless is arrived and form'd
>   in you,
> You are henceforth secure, whatever comes or goes.

But *identity* (and its cognates) also has other meanings in
Whitman's poems, and in "Song of Myself" especially: the poet
(or his *persona*) identifies himself with other people—
sometimes even with inanimate things or abstractions—by such
strong empathy that he feels himself to be, for the moment,
that person or thing. Not only does he see all people in himself,
but he imaginatively and compassionately becomes each of
these in turn as they come into the focus of his sympathy:

> Agonies are one of my changes of garments,
> I do not ask the wounded person how he feels, I myself
>   become the wounded person,
> My hurt turns livid upon me as I lean on a cane and observe.[24]

As a consequence of this omnivorous identification, the *persona* of "Song of Myself" undergoes many metamorphoses,
though the *self* itself does not change; it merely "changes gar-
ments," occupations, and habitat. And change of habitat gives
vision. This word also has several connotations in Whitman's

poems. It means, first of all, *seeing,* and the voyeuristic "I" of "Song of Myself" travels with the speed of a dream over the earth, embracing all it sees by his voluptuous sight, and even beyond the earth; walking in space "with the tender and growing night" (sec. 21), visiting "the orchards of spheres" and looking at the "quintillions" of planets ripened and "quintillions green" (sec. 33); ascending from the moon (sec. 49) and perceiving that the glimmering moonlight on the earth is "noonday sunbeams reflected," and by analogy debouching "to the steady and central from the offspring great or small." This is Whitman's "vision" in its broadest, most ambiguous, and "mystical" sense: by intuition he has penetrated, he says, metaphorically, to the fountainhead of existence—the moonlight symbolizing the divine energy reflected in physical existences. (*Cf.* Emerson's doctrine of "correspondences.") In section 27 the poet asks, "To be in any form, what is that?" Then he answers the *how* rather than the *what*: "Round and round we go, all of us, and ever come back thither"; every existence is fated to tread the round of birth, growth, death—and rebirth ("and ever come back thither"). This is the great insight (vision) of the poet in "Song of Myself." The grass grows luxuriantly from the "white heads of old mothers" and "the dead young men and women" (see sec. 6):

They are alive and well somewhere,
The smallest sprout shows there is really no death,
And if ever there was it led forward life, and does
    not wait at the end to arrest it,
And ceas'd the moment life appear'd.

All goes onward and outward, nothing collapses,
And to die is different from what anyone supposed,
    and luckier.

Sexual contact quivers the poet-*persona* "to a new identity" (sec. 28). The transfer of the seed from the father to the mother is a "perpetual payment" of life on a "perpetual loan." All forms of living things go through the inevitable cycle, but sex keeps the visible world constantly prolific, vital, and beautiful (sec. 29). By visualizing the miracle by which the landscapes of the world are kept "full-sized and golden" by this eternal process of renewal, the poet becomes reconciled to death, which is but a long sleep (sec. 50). The meaning of this cycle is a mystery beyond logical comprehension—"a word unsaid ... not in any dictionary"—but:

> Something it swings on more than the earth swings on,
> To it the creation is the friend whose embracing awakes me.

This transcendent "something," which is to the life-and-death cycle as gravitation is to the earth, is "not chaos or death," but "form, union, plan ... eternal life ... happiness." This riddle is strikingly similar to the Hindu doctrine of transmigration, especially in section 51:

> The past and present wilt—I have fill'd them, emptied them,
> And proceed to fill the next fold of the future.

But section 51 also has other subtle implications. The protagonist of the poem is nearing the end of his identifications and journeys across space and through time. Imaginatively and symbolically he has filled and exhausted each niche of time and space visited (and visualized) in the poem; but though his poem must end and he, man-poet, must die, through his poem he can continue in the future to speak intimately to each reader:

Listener up there! what have you to confide to me?
Look in my face while I snuff the sidle of evening,
(Talk honestly, no one else hears you, and I stay only
   a minute longer.)

So thoroughly has the poet identified himself with his book that it scarcely matters whether the "I" breathing the "sidle of evening" (the darkness coming on) is the man anticipating his death or the *persona* whose visit with his reader must soon end with the last line of the poem. This is the advantage of Whitman's symbolical language: it can suggest far more than it says. From the grass as fertility symbol at the beginning of "Song of Myself" to the grass under which the singer of the song is buried at the end (but still a voice speaking to the reader from under his boot-soles), this poem is an exploration of what it means—and how it feels—to be a "human identity" in the eternal cycle of being.

5

This summary of Whitman's *identification* practices in "Song of Myself" differs radically from D. H. Lawrence's interpretation of what he calls Whitman's "merging."[25] Because the poet says he "aches with amorous love" and is attracted as by gravitation to everyone he meets, Lawrence hurls sarcasm at him:

Your Moby Dick must be really dead. That lovely phallic monster of the individual you. Dead mentalized.

I know only that my body doesn't by any means gravitate to all I meet or know. I find I can shake hands with a few people. But most I wouldn't touch with a long prop.

Your mainspring is broken, Walt Whitman. The mainspring

of your own individuality. And so you run down with a great whirr, merging with everything.

You have killed your isolate Moby Dick. You have mentalized your deep sensual body, and that's the death of it.

I am everything and everything is me and so we're all One in One Identity, like the Mundane Egg, which had been addled quite a while.[26]

So instead of sensualizing the soul, as Edwin Miller claims, Lawrence says Whitman has "mentalized" it. He wants to merge with anybody and everything because he is in love with death. As for his *self*:

Oh, Walter, Walter, what have you done with it? What have you done with yourself? With your own individual self? For it sounds as if it had all leaked out of you, leaked into the universe.

Post mortem effects. The individuality had leaked out of him.[27]

Frederik Schyberg took this criticism in his *Walt Whitman* (1933) and applied it more specifically to Whitman's psychology: because Whitman was by nature homosexual and alienated from the mores of his society, he never found happiness in sexual love, for which he substituted fantasy love affairs with men.[28] Unable to imagine a satisfying physical love, he poetized a divine love beyond life. Love and death are inextricably associated in his poems. With the biographical part of this theory Edwin H. Miller agrees, for he says that Whitman's regression in his poetry "in order to capture the child's construction of reality" imposed a limitation on his "love vision":

As the body, or the "I", quiescently accepts the soul's sexual invasion, so his vision cannot go beyond his (feminine) passivity and his dependent nature. Except for a few flamboyant passages of erotic aggressiveness, Whitman establishes a passive relationship with his imaginary and real lovers. Even in art Whitman could not escape his fearful shrinking from normal sexuality, or cross "bridges" he was unable to cross in life.[29]

The critics who emphasize Whitman's "mystical insight" do not necessarily reject this biological (or psychoanalytical) interpretation, but they mainly ignore it for the larger philosophical insights they find. James E. Miller calls "Song of Myself" an example of "inverted mystical experience,"[30] by which he means that the poet attained his illumination without passing through the preliminary stages Evelyn Underhill describes in *Mysticism: A Study in the Nature and Development of Man's Spiritual Consciousness* (1920). In other words, he attained his mystical insight not by asceticism but "through the transfigured senses":

In "Song of Myself" the self is not, as in the traditional mystical experience, submerged or annihilated, but rather celebrated; the senses are not humbled but glorified. When the soul plunges his tongue to the "bare-stript heart" of the poet, the physical becomes transfigured into the spiritual, the body from beard to feet is held in the grip of the soul, and the body and soul become one: "Lack one lacks both." The imagery of the tongue and heart is ingenious: the spiritual tongue informs; the physical heart receives. Such imagery suggests that it is only through the intimate fusion of the physical and spiritual, the ennobling of the physical through the spiritual, that one can know transcendent reality.[31]

The difference between the two Millers is in emphasis: James E. looks to the "transfigured senses," Edwin H. to the "sensualizing of the soul." Of course, too, as a nonpsychoanalytical critic, James E. Miller does not share Lawrence's attitude to Whitman's "merging" in his poems, and regards his "'Calamus' idea" as "brotherly love . . . a basic Christian concept . . . indispensable to the democratic ideal."[32]

A critic with a position somewhere between Lawrence and the two Millers is the late Richard Chase. In his *Walt Whitman Reconsidered* (1955) he calls "Song of Myself" "a profound and lovely comic drama of the self":

> The comic spirit of the poem is of the characteristic American sort, providing expression for a realism at once naturalistic and transcendental, for the wit, gaiety, and festive energy of all good comedy, and also for meditative soliloquy, at once intensely personal and strongly generic.[33]

Thus Whitman "plays a losing game with ironical realism." The juxtaposition of transcendental idealism and realistic "self-metamorphoses" in a loose structure of almost free association gives the "Song of Myself" an "incongruous diversity" and undercuts the serious moral purpose.[34] Chase compares Whitman's protagonist "self" to Henry James's Christopher Newman in *The American*, who had the "look of being committed to nothing in particular, of standing in an attitude of general hospitality to the chances of life."[35] In fact, Chase believes that the "self" of "Song of Myself" is "a character portrayed in a recognizable American way; it illustrates the fluid, unformed personality exulting alternately in its provisional attempts to define itself and in its sense that it has no definition."[36]

But "Song of Myself" is a failure only on Whitman's moral terms; in Chase's terms of "comedy" it is a great success. He praises Whitman also for making "sex a possible subject of

American literature," and says that in section 5 "love is at once
. . . sublimely generalized and perfectly particularized" (words
that almost contradict Chase's thesis). He also finds nothing
else in the "grandiose nineteenth-century melodrama of love
and death" to compare with "the delicate precision" of Whitman's elegiac ending of his "Song." Furthermore, "Whitman's
relation of the self to the rest of the universe is a successful
aesthetic or compositional device, whatever we may think of
it as a moral assertion."[37] The latter—or the "paradox of
'identity' "—is the crux; Whitman says that he sings himself
but assumes that all selves are (or can be) the same as his.
Unfortunately, "Whitman loses his sense that his metaphor of
self vs. en masse* is a *paradox*, that self and en-masse are in
dialectical opposition."

> Both politically and by nature man has "identity", in two senses
> of the word; on the one hand, he is integral in himself, unique,
> and separate; on the other hand, he is equal to, or even the same
> as everyone else. Like the Concord transcendentalists, Whitman
> was easily led in prophetic moods to generalize the second term
> of the paradox of identity beyond the merely human world and
> with his ruthless equalitarianism to conceive the All, a vast
> cosmic democracy, placid, without episode, separation or conflict,
> though suffused, perhaps, with a bland illumination. More than
> anything else, it is this latter tendency which finally ruined
> Whitman as a poet, submerging as it did, his chief forte and
> glory—his entirely original, vividly realistic presentation of the
> comedy and pathos of "the single separate person."[38]

Balzac called Cooper's Natty Bumppo, who also happened to
be one of Whitman's favorite characters in fiction, "a magnificent moral hermaphrodite, born between the savage and the

---

* See the *Inscription* poem "One's-Self I Sing."

civilized states of man."[39] Chase says Natty "was a spiritual
father of Walt Whitman." Like Bumppo, Whitman rejected
his contemporary society for a pastoral world of innocence and
freedom—"a prelapsarian world." However, this critic does not
find Whitman's pastoral world as romantic and nostalgic as
Melville's, Mark Twain's, or Hemingway's, agreeing that:

> Whitman's utopian rejection of society is under modern condi-
> tions the necessary first step toward the preservation of what is
> vital in society and the revitalization of what is not, and, further-
> more, that despite his intellectual short-comings, despite even
> the final disappearance of his idealism into the All, Whitman
> knew more of the homely root facts of the life of modern society
> than did Melville or Mark Twain, and that at his best his vision
> stubbornly began and ended with these root facts.[40]

The strength and charm of Chase's ambivalent praise of
"Song of Myself" is his relating Whitman's art to nineteenth-
century American literature and culture, including the unin-
hibited vitality of American humor, the paradoxes of individual-
ism in a democratic society, and the problems of a self-made
personality. Instead of "mysticism" and philosophy of the self,
he finds amusing quirkiness, the language of the "tall tale," and
comic postures. (Chase acknowledges his debt to Constance
Rourke,[41] who made some of the same points about Whitman
in her *American Humor*, 1931.) But the mythic poet of *Leaves
of Grass* was an embarrassment to Chase, and he thought
Whitman was deluded and distracted by transcendental dual-
ism (in thought) and symbolism (in art). Unfortunately, it
was only in "Song of Myself" that Whitman stumbled into the
magnificent role of American comic poet, by turns Dionysian,
Rabelaisian, and satirical.

The contradictions that Chase finds in Whitman's poems, V. K. Chari resolves by Vedantic psychology and philosophy in *Whitman in the Light of Vedantic Mysticism* (1964). Others have found Vedantic parallels in *Leaves of Grass*, but Dr. Chari was the first to bring to the study of this subject an intimate knowledge of the whole Vedantic literature. He makes no attempt in his book to account for Whitman's surprising familiarity with Vedantic perceptions, though he does suggest that he got hints from essays and poems of Emerson, who had some knowledge of Vedantic thought. Chari's primary effort is to show that many of Whitman's paradoxes and ambiguities become intelligible "in the light of Vedantic mysticism," which reveals a consistent unity in his whole poetic experience:

> Mysticism, as it is understood by the Vedantist, and as it finds expression in Whitman, is a way of embracing the "other"—the objective world—in an inclusive conception of the self. In other words, it is a way of finding the world in the self and as the self, thus negating the opposition of the me and the not-me. It is the power to "enter upon all, and incorporate them into himself or herself," as Whitman has expressed it in a slightly different context ["Thoughts"]. It is such an expansive, dynamic, and exultant conception of the self that constitutes the central element of meaning in *Leaves of Grass*. Any interpretation of Whitman must take note of this unified point of view that lends cohesion and consistency to his poetry. Though Whitman made no attempt to formulate a philosophy, his writings spring from a unity of poetic experience. The whole of his poetic effort was centered in the exploration of the nature of the self.[42]

Like James E. Miller and Malcolm Cowley, Chari believes that Whitman had experienced "mysticism" before writing his 1855 poems, but he disagrees with Miller that "Song of Myself" gives a clear progression of " 'entry into the mystical state' (the first phase) to emergence from it (the last phase)"; and with Cowley that the poem is "arranged in the narrative order of a 'moment of ecstasy' followed by a sequel. . . ." Rather, the ecstasy described in section 5 is "in retrospect." Exactly how retrospective Chari does not try to establish precisely, though he finds in Whitman's juvenile poetry and prose, and especially in his pre-LG notebooks, the introspection and self-dissatisfaction which was the equivalent of Evelyn Underhill's "dark night of the soul" that James E. Miller could not find, causing him to call Whitman's mysticism "inverted." Chari says:

> Whitman's intense self-awareness might have sprung from the early autoerotic emotions of his boyhood and a primary narcissism. But it manifested itself as a certain habit of mentally returning upon himself, of reflecting upon his own inner processes. Whitman was a dreamy boy, a languid mystical type, with a lazy, contemplative habit of mind. He was exceptionally susceptible to his physical and spiritual environment. His own mystical inclination was aided by the strong religious proclivities of his paternal family, who were followers of Quakerism, and the boy's early training, in the belief in the "inner light," made him all the more receptive to "quietism" and predisposed him to a mystical life. The "child" who went forth every day becoming the object he looked upon showed a wonderful capacity for intuitive identification. . . . [He] . . . felt no barriers between the universe and his soul, each flowed into the other, each interpenetrated the other.[43]

Although Whitman's "emergent ego" led him to the discovery of his "mystic identity," a long process of sublimation preceded his writing the 1855 poems. His discovery, aided by his reading of Emerson, Coleridge, Carlyle, and perhaps Hindu literature in translation,[44] was that, as Whitman expressed it in an unpublished note, "behind all faculties of the human being, as the sight, the other senses and even the emotions and the intellect stands the real power, the *mystical identity, the real I or Me or You* [Chari's italics]."[45]

In his introspection, reading, and notebook jottings, Whitman was searching for his "real I or Me." Chari finds it significant that at this stage he became a passive spectator, like the "self as *sáksi* or the detached percipience." Section 4 of "Song of Myself" describes the self "which witnesses and waits while the endless spectacle of the world goes by . . .":

Trippers and askers surround me,
People I meet, the effect upon me of my early life
   or the ward and city I live in, or the nation,
The latest dates, discoveries, inventions, societies,
   authors old and new,
My dinner, dress, associates, looks, compliments, dues,
The real or fancied indifference of some man or woman
   I love,
The sickness of one of my folks or myself, or ill-doing
   or loss or lack of money, or depressions or exaltations,
Battles, the horrors of fratricidal war, the fever of
   doubtful news, the fitful events;
These come to me days and nights and go from me again,
But they are not the Me myself.

Apart from the pulling and hauling stands what I am,
Stands amused, complacent, compassionating, idle, unitary,
Looks down, is erect, or bends an arm on an impalpable
   certain rest,
Looking with side-curved head curious what will come next,

Both in and out of the game and watching and wondering at it.

Backward I see in my own days where I sweated through
    fog with linguists and contenders,
I have no mockings or arguments, I witness and wait.

Whitman's "Me myself," which stands apart, observing and evaluating the affairs of his personal and public life, resembles the "Dynamic Self" of Vedanticism, or the Brahman of the Upanishad. Out of his "emergent ego" eventually developed this deeper or "real" self, the self of expansion and enlargement:

Following on self-knowledge comes the consciousness that "I am all." Since identification or expansion is a centrifugal movement, it gives rise to an internal dynamism; limitless pools of energy are released from within, and they result in creative activity. This phase marks the return of the spirit from its inner recess into the world of dynamic activity, even as it is inevitably followed by a return to itself—withdrawal and self-immersion.

Whitman the cosmic poet is the creative phase of the self; *Leaves of Grass* is the embodiment. The work has grown out of an irresistible urge for creation. The poet and the book are identical. "Camerado, this is no book, / Who touches this touches a man." The work is an outcropping of the poet's personality, the emanation of his vital, dynamic self.[46]

Self-knowledge and enlargement of consciousness gave Whitman "a tremendous flow of vital energy." He declares that he is "infinite and omnigenous" and feels himself to be "a god and creator." The "I" of "Song of Myself" (sec. 41) outbids the gods of antique religions, calling them "old cautious hucksters,"

Accepting the rough deific sketches to fill out better
   in myself, bestowing them freely on each man and
     woman I see, . . .
The supernatural of no account, myself waiting my time
   to be one of the supremes,
The day of getting ready for me when I shall do as
   much good as the best, and be as prodigious;
By my life-lumps! becoming already a creator,
Putting myself here and now to the ambush'd womb
   of the shadows.

In the context of Vedantic mysticism, this expansiveness of imagination comes from Whitman's attaining "cosmic consciousness." In Chase's context of American culture, it is the exuberant hyperbole of comedy—and in his enthusiasm the poet does resort to incongruous (or deliberately jarring) colloquial emphasis: "By my life-lumps!" The contexts of these two critics give diametrically opposite readings. The comic reading is an unsympathetic interpretation of the meditation and "identification" which Whitman strove for. That he did strive for it is shown by his Yoga-like mental exercises, as when he instructs himself in a note:

Abstract yourself from this book; realize where you are at present located, the point you stand that is now to you the centre of all. Look up overhead, *think of space stretching out, think of all the unnumbered orbs wheeling safely there* [Chari's italics], invisible to us by day, some visible by night. . . . Spend some minutes faithfully in this exercise. Then again realize yourself upon the earth, at the particular point you now occupy . . . [thinks of four directions]. Seize these firmly in your mind, *pass freely over immense distances*. Turn your face a moment thither. Fix defi-

nitely the direction and the idea of the distances of separate sections of your own country, also of England, the Mediterranean
sea, Cape Horn, the North Pole, and such like distant places.[47]

In Roja Yoga, Chari points out, the ultimate achievement of
meditation is "complete dissolution of the mind," but Whitman practiced his self-taught Yoga only to attain consciousness
of his identity with "the world-all."[48] This process Chari calls
"the paradox of identity." In Whitman's poems on the self,
such as "Song of Myself" and "The Sleepers," he dramatizes
"the activity of the dynamic self." The paradox is stasis in
motion. For example, "Song of Myself" is permeated by images
of movement, progression, succession, but they eventually are
seen from a stationary point of observation:

> Strange as it may seem, the perpetual symbolic voyages and end-
> less processions constantly refer back to the "still point" at the
> center. This central paradox of fixity in motion and oneness in
> the many is implicit in Whitman's conception of the self. Whit-
> man sees the whole universe as but an emanation of the creative
> self: "The universe is in myself—it shall pass through me as a
> procession." And again, "Through me the afflatus surging and
> surging, through me the current and index."[49]

This doctrine that "The universe is in myself . . ." is a kind
of philosophical idealism, but it has been misunderstood, Chari
says; indeed, Whitman misunderstood it to the extent of thinking that "German idealism," especially the philosophy of
Hegel, was *his* philosophy.[50] This idealism "denies reality to
objects and regards them as ideas or apparitions." The extreme
idealism of Hegel asserts that the existing object is nothing but
a "conflux of ideas or universals." Since Vedanta holds that
"the world is non-existent apart from Brahman," many West-

ern readers think it denies the reality of the physical world, but, Chari maintains, Vedanta has "a realistic core," a realistic epistemology. Because the objective world is not independent of Brahman, "it is not ultimate." Yet it exists, nevertheless, in its own relative position.

Whitman never renounced his earliest (1847) notebook credo:

> I am the poet of reality,
> I say the earth is not an echo,
> Nor man an apparition;
> But all the things seen are real,
> The witness and albic dawn of things real
> And the world is no joke,
> Nor any part of it a sham.[51]

In spite of this faith in the reality of things seen and felt, Whitman claims "Idealism" as "the proper guide for New World metaphysics":[52]

The type of idealism Whitman envisages is of a mystical, transcendental brand, in which the "religious tone, the consciousness of mystery, the recognition of the future, of the unknown, of Deity over and under all, and of the divine purpose, are never absent," of which the unknown spiritual world is an essential ingredient. Such an idealism, according to Whitman, serves as a counterpoise to "the growing excess and arrogance of realism," the modern worship of facts; it will rise above the visible material nature to "superior and spiritual points of view," and indicates that man's destination is "beyond the ostensible, the mortal." For Whitman spirit is the foundation of the world. The visible universe is rooted in the invisible; spirituality underlies all existence: ". . . the pervading invisible fact of life here . . . furnishing . . . only permanent and unitary meaning to all." When he declares that the unseen soul is "the real, / (purport of all these apparitions of the real)" ["Thou Mother with Thy Equal Brood"], Whitman echoes faithfully the Upanishadic utterance which describes the *brahman* as "real of the real" and avers that all creatures have their roots in the *sat* (being). Emerson, too, claims that "the foundations of man are not in matter but in spirit."[53]

Whitman is thus "in perfect accord with the Vedantist," and his idealism, "as also the Vedantist's, is more correctly characterized as mystical or *transcendental realism*." Of course, the Vedantist hopes eventually to achieve transcendence into the formless Absolute. This, too, seems to have been Whitman's ultimate hope, for in old age he wanted to end his "books with thoughts, or radiations from thoughts, on death, immortality, and a free entrance into the spiritual world."[54] In fantasy, at least, he made that "free entrance" in "Passage to India"—and "more than India . . . the seas of God."

6

The great problem in interpreting the poems of *Leaves of Grass* is to find a suitable context, some pattern of ideas, philosophy, religion, or psychology in which such terms as "self," "soul," "spirit," "identity," "sex," "death," etc., have interrelated meaning. The fact that the context is necessary proves that the poems do have a unity of some kind, but the unity is so subjective that there is always the danger that each critic, by applying his own subjective context, will find whatever meaning he wishes. That this has happened over and over again, the long, turbulent course of Whitman criticism shows unmistakably.

To V. K. Chari the context is Vedantic mysticism, and he

has a strong argument in favor of this context in the similarity of many of Whitman's terms and symbols to those of Vedanticism—and there is a possibility that the poet may have derived them directly from translations of Indian literature.[55] But Whitman's poems are neither Vedic scriptures nor commentary on them by a Sankara. The question is, how much meaning is added or left out by interpreting *Leaves of Grass* in the context of Vedantic mysticism? And the same question can be asked about Edwin H. Miller's psychoanalytical context. Does "regression" explain everything of value in Whitman's poems—or in his art? Chase's interpretation of "Song of Myself" as a comic poem supplies a context which the poet obviously did not intend—though in some passages he was deliberately ironical, satirical, self-mocking—so that, if he was a comic poet, it was inadvertent or only in a fleeting mood. Similarly, O. K. Nambiar finds a Yoga context in *Walt Whitman and Yoga*, and again in many passages the Yoga concepts seem appropriate.[56] Less surprising, James E. Miller, Karl Shapiro, and Bernice Slote in *Start with the Sun* find a common "tradition"[57] for Whitman, D. H. Lawrence, Hart Crane, Dylan Thomas, Henry Miller, and other "cosmic" poets.

It was almost inevitable that a poet so usable (in Herman Melville's sense of "usable past") would be discovered by Existentialist criticism. And this, as of the present moment, is the latest contribution. Professor E. F. Carlisle is writing a book on the subject, and his essay "Walt Whitman: Drama of Identity" is a preliminary sample. By Existentialism is meant the philosophy of Karl Jaspers and Martin Buber, but especially the latter's epistemology of "identity" ("I and Thou") and "this-world theology."

Carlisle begins his interpretation of *Leaves of Grass* by agreeing with a host of older critics that "The main theme of the poetry is the discovery of identity."[58] But he does not believe that Whitman found identity by sublimation of his neurotic sexuality, or in a "death-wish," or "earth mysticism" (anticipating D. H. Lawrence), or in Vedantic "cosmic consciousness." He found it in an "interaction between self and the external world":

> In a general sense, this interaction might have several explanations—from the completely naturalistic (the material world is the primary reality and the self is absorbed into it) to the completely idealistic (the self or mind is the primary reality and the world is an unreal appearance). In Leaves of Grass the dialogue that poem after poem dramatizes involves a reciprocal or mutual relationship between the self and world. To engage in such a dialogue the self must transcend its limits and isolation as a simple separate ego or as an alienated man. In a very general sense, Identity emerges as Whitman discovers meaning for himself through dialogue. Sometimes a poem presents a failure to establish dialogue, either because the self seems sufficient to itself, or because one of the many threats to the emergence, survival, and triumph of personality or identity prevails. Both the crises of personality and its successes show that the dramatic interplay of self with the world constitutes the central action of Leaves of Grass.[59]

In the terminology of Buber, the interaction of the self with the world takes place by "transcendence" and "dialogue." "Transcendence" does not mean, as in Vedantic mysticism or American Transcendentalism, a passing from the physical realm of existence to a purely spiritual or metaphysical realm, but simply a " 'going beyond' or 'rising above' the simple, separated, sometimes alienated self and the dilemmas and divisions that self faces as isolated man."[60] In his poems Whitman strives constantly to immerse his self in "physical reality, in history, in death or suffering" without being overcome—to rise above these, but on a human and not a supernatural level. The means of establishing this relation between the self and the empirical is by "dialogue," or realizing Buber's "I-Thou" relation. "Thou" includes all that is Not-Me: nature, the physical world, things, as well as other persons or selves. *Reality* is not in the self but in the *interhuman* realm between the self and the world, or between one self and another self. "Buber suggests that man grasps his complete humanity only in this fundamental reciprocity. The relationship, however, cannot be sustained; for one normally has only momentary or transitory experiences of mutuality. Thus, the experience is dynamic—that is, it consists of a series of repeated actions."[61]

Some critics regard Whitman's poems as monologues. Carlisle mentions R. W. B. Lewis (*Trials of the Word*, p. 35), who says Whitman "was above all the poet of the self and of the self's swaying motion—outward into a teeming world where objects were 'strung like beads of glory' on his sight; backward into private communion with the 'real Me.' "[62] (If Carlisle had read Edwin H. Miller, he might have mentioned his "regression" theory.) "For Lewis, when Whitman stopped writing as the solitary singer, he stopped writing valuable poetry. In my view, Whitman never was a singer of solitude except in those poems in which dialogue failed, nor was his public or communal interest destructive of him as a poet."[63] This is the most radical aspect of Carlisle's interpretation: he accepts the whole of *Leaves of Grass* as a unity, the "program" along with the "poems"—not that the poems are of equal value, but he judges them not aesthetically but in their success or failure to establish "dialogue."

This Existentialist critic finds "three basic relationships or modes of transcendence" in Whitman's poems; that is, three forms of dialogue leading the poet's "persona to more complete awareness of the self in the world (not above or beyond or withdrawn from it) and to a fuller grasping of his humanity." These are:

(1) a dialogue between self and empirical reality, or the external, physical world—"There Was a Child Went Forth" dramatizes this mode; (2) a dialogue between self and other, or another and others—"Children of Adam" and "Calamus" develop these relationships; (3) a dialogue between self and spirit, or death and spirit—"Crossing Brooklyn Ferry," "Out of the Cradle Endlessly Rocking," and "When Lilacs Last in the Dooryard Bloom'd" present this third mode of transcendence.[64]

In a few poems, "Whitman does sometimes dramatize the sort of transcendental experience which requires idealistic or mystic conceptions for explanation—or at least allows them as reasonably valid alternatives," such as "Passage to India," and possibly "The Mystic Trumpeter" and "Joy Shipmate Joy." However, in the two latter poems "transcendence" becomes more a state of being than a process. But in most of his poems such hierarchies as "Ideal, noumenal, or spiritual world" are "unreal because of the empirical and historical." The experience "at the center of *Leaves of Grass* is human experience."[65]

In "As I Ebb with the Ocean of Life" the *persona* is estranged and in despair, and has not established a dialogue with the world he faces. "As the poem develops, however, that dialogue *is* established and the poet is truly 'both in and out of the game.'" Carlisle thinks that Jaspers's statement, " 'I break through it [the actual world] in order to return to it out of the experience of Transcendence, at one and the same time in and out of it' (*Reason and Existenz*, p. 94), could provide an interesting gloss to Whitman's line."[66] In "There Was a Child Went Forth" the young consciousness "enters into a material relation with the world, a dialogue in which reality lies neither in the boy or the world but in between . . . people are objects, not yet other persons."[67]

In "Children of Adam" we find "sexual dialogue . . . sex becomes an act of the complete man—blood and brain together —an act that reveals one possibility for authentic dialogue." The "Children of Adam" poems celebrate "sexual love which reaches fulfillment." In some of the "Calamus" poems we have "a tension between isolation, or fear of it, and the confidence and security a 'you and I' relationship brings." In general, "the 'Calamus' love moves away from guilt and shame, toward a mutual reciprocal relation between the 'I' and his comrade, and finally to a sense of community brotherhood (see, for example, 'Of the Terrible Doubt of Appearances' and 'The Base of All Metaphysics.' "[68] One of the poems which most completely dramatize "full communication with others and with spirit" is "Crossing Brooklyn Ferry." In the context of the poem, Carlisle thinks, "soul" has an Existentialist meaning of "the self experienced totally in a lived historical moment."

It might seem that only idealistic conceptions could explain the Whitmanian dialogue of self and spirit, but not so. The distinction is a fine one, yet possible. The speaker in "Crossing Brooklyn Ferry" realizes a common identity within actual human experience and not initially beyond it. The end of the poem does not simply mean that natural facts are signs of spiritual ones; it suggests, instead, that the meaning of experience is not imposed either by the self or by some objective standard from without. Meaning arises only in the lived moment—in the sphere of the interhuman where the poet discovers the essential "we" unfolding in existence and in the poem.[69]

But of course Whitman's major "drama of identity" is "Song of Myself," which also dramatizes the central action of *Leaves of Grass*: the dialogue of the self with the world. The poem begins with "unitary self," moves to an incomplete dialogue of the self and not-self, and "ends in unity—in full mutuality as the self and the world merge or become one. As the poem develops, it dramatizes awareness, vision, and journey which transcend time and space." In the process, the "I" or *persona* discovers "a 'real Me' whose awareness expands as he becomes others." The union of body and soul (sec. 5) originates a "new sensibility." The catalogues "define the extension of awareness." A crisis of identity is reached in section 37, when the "poet-hero" is reduced to virtual defeat by "the dying, the suffering, the victims," but "on the verge of a usual mistake" (sec. 38) that "he has lighted the surfaces and the 'down-hearted doubters' too much. From here on, he will celebrate the emergence of the authentic self as he attempts to embrace physical and spiritual reality as one." In section 41 the *persona* "assumes the roles of bard and prophet," offering "the total experience of a whole man, not the old ideals of duality."[70]

To read this "unity" in terms of Emerson's Over-Soul is too limiting:

The modern voice of Walt Whitman dramatizes, instead, transcendence as stages of conscious participation in all levels of being. This voice, speaking to modern man of awareness and transcendence, makes the individual a force who acts and is not merely acted upon. *Leaves of Grass* affirms the self, but that self is not isolated and does not capitulate to the force of society or to necessity, fate, chaos, or despair—to the threats which might obliterate his positive identity. The hero of *Leaves of Grass* defies such limitations and struggles to expand his consciousness in order to transcend without denying his own historical existence. . . . He asserts, actually, the absolute need to confront the whole of human existence.[71]

As mentioned above, Professor Carlisle's essay is only a brief introduction to the book he is writing on Whitman and the problem of identity, and this summary still further truncates his interpretation, which promises a drastic reversal in Whitman criticism: finding unity instead of fragmentation or incompletion in the poet's life-work, and a justification for the poetry on the basis of Whitman's socio-religious "program," which to many critics in recent years has been an embarrassment. In his published condensation of his interpretation, Professor Carlisle has said almost nothing about the poems as poetry, as aesthetic experience. Possibly he means to take Whitman at his word and not attempt to "get at" his poems as art, but only as *total experience* of, in Whitman's words, "a full-sized man." On this basis, *Leaves of Grass* may, after all, be regarded as "A Bible for Democracy."

V FORM AND STRUCTURE

My form has strictly grown from my purports and facts,
and is the analogy of them.

—1876 Preface

1

One of the reviewers of the first *Leaves of Grass* quoted in Chapter I said that the poems were "neither in rhyme nor blank verse, but in a sort of excited prose broken into lines without any attempt at measure or regularity . . ."[1] This was the typical reaction of Whitman's contemporaries to his revolutionary verse-form and structure, for they were so accustomed to rhyme and meter in poetry that they thought any composition without them was not *poetry*. Whitman tacitly admitted that this attitude still prevailed in 1882 when he wrote his generous tribute to the memory of Longfellow, who had recently died:

> Longfellow in his voluminous works seems to me not only to be eminent in the style and forms of poetical expression that mark the present age (an idiosyncrasy, almost a sickness, of

verbal melody), but to bring what is always dearest as poetry to the general human heart and taste . . . To the ungracious complaint-charge of his want of racy nativity and special originality, I shall only say that America and the world may well be reverently thankful . . . I have heard Longfellow himself say, that ere the New World can be worthily original, and announce herself and her own heroes, she must be well saturated with the originality of others, and respectfully consider the heroes that lived before Agamemnon.[2]

Yet, in spite of his great respect for Longfellow, Whitman had attempted to write poetry which was in many ways the antithesis of Longfellow's: so "original" that it was revolutionary, presenting an archetypal New World "hero," and with robust harmonics little resembling the "verbal melody" of Longfellow. Whitman tried his hand at the 'sick melodies' his contemporaries preferred, before turning his back on them in 1855. He had done so because he believed the New World poet must have his own forms and structures, "transcendent and new"; that "poems distilled from other poems [as Longfellow's certainly were] must pass away."[3]

But however original his "new forms" might be, the general theory on which Whitman rationalized them was not new. Emerson had declared in his essay "The Poet" that "it is not metres, but a metre-making argument that makes a poem,—a thought so passionate and alive that like the spirit of a plant or an animal it has an architecture of its own, and adorns nature with a new thing."[4] Whitman rephrased this doctrine in his 1855 Preface, but kept the biological analogy:

The poetic quality is not marshalled in rhyme or uniformity . . . The profit of rhyme is that it drops seeds of a sweeter and more luxuriant rhyme, and of uniformity that it conveys itself into its own roots in the ground out of sight. The rhyme and uniformity of perfect poems show the free growth of metrical laws and bud from them as unerringly and loosely as lilacs or roses on a bush, and take shapes as compact as the shapes of chestnuts and oranges and melons and pears, and shed the perfume impalpable to form. The fluency and ornaments of the finest poems or music or oratory or recitations are not independent but dependent.[5]

Coleridge, to whom both Emerson and Whitman were indebted, had expressed this "organic theory" with more precision in his lecture on "Shakespeare, a Poet Generally":

The form is mechanic, when on any given material we impress a pre-determined form, not necessarily arising out of the properties of the material;—as when to a mass of wet clay we give whatever shape we wish it to retain when hardened. The organic form, on the other hand, is innate; it shapes, as it develops, itself from within, and the fullness of its development is one and the same with the perfection of its outward form. Such as the life is, such is the form. Nature, the prime genial artist, inexhaustible in diverse powers, is equally inexhaustible in forms;—each exterior is the physiognomy of the being within,—its true image reflected and thrown out from the concave mirror;—and even such is the appropriate excellence of her chosen poet.[6]

Coleridge used this aesthetic concept to distinguish a real *poem* from mere verse: "a legitimate poem must be one, the parts of which mutually support and explain each other; all in their proportion harmonizing with, and supporting the purpose and known influence of metrical arrangement."[7] In other words, the meter, diction, imagery, etc., must all work together for the desired effect—a concept which Poe borrowed from Coleridge in his criticism but forgot or ignored in writing "The Raven," in which the comical sound effects work against the subject matter. The application of Coleridge's distinction between a *poem* and *verse* has had enormous beneficial influence in twentieth-century literary criticism, but his "organic" theory was scarcely more than a poetic "conceit" in the adaptation of it by Emerson and Whitman. The idea of "forget the rules and conventions and let the poem find its own expression" does neatly summarize Whitman's practice in general in *Leaves of Grass*, but the analogy between a poem and a growing plant is illogical, implying that all the poet has to do is plant the seed in fertile soil (his own consciousness) and let it grow like any other organic form in the biological realm of existence. But in reality the poet not only plants the sperm in his own consciousness, where it may take root and begin to grow, a process in which he is both father and mother; he must himself give the poem life, shape it like God creating Eve out of Adam's rib. Of course, a few poems do seem to emerge out of their creator's subconscious and to take shape without the poet's conscious effort, like Coleridge's "Kubla Khan." Some of Whitman's poems may have originated in and been partly written by the aid of his subconscious, but no one who studies his manuscripts can believe that he got more than an impulse, an occasional image, the germ of a poem, from what used to be called "inspiration." Whitman was a "maker" in the literal sense of the term, shaping, experimenting, and revising incessantly until he had achieved a structure in language which satisfied his rational judgment.

There is, of course, a similarity between Coleridge's "organic form" and Whitman's expressing his intuition so that his objective structure (words on paper) harmonized with the *idea* in his mind; but the difference is that his poem grows not by some mysterious *élan vital* of its own but by means of the poet's combined emotional and thinking processes. A better term for

Whitman's medium for achieving his intuition would be *expressive form*. This term is also ambiguous and has been used in various senses, but applied to *Leaves of Grass* it means that Whitman began (usually) not with a predetermined rhythmical and linguistic pattern but with an indefinite striving to discover a form in the very process of giving expression to his idea or intuition. (The psychology of this process is extremely complex and variable but need not be explored to understand the rudiments of Whitman's prosodic techniques.)

Whitman's prosody is usually labeled "free verse," but all this term tells us is that the poem is not in rhyme and meter. His verse was free in this sense, and it is of some significance that Remy de Gourmont thought French *vers libre* owed its origin to him (through Vielé-Griffin).[8] But *expressive form* tells more about the nature and function of Whitman's poetic form than does its freedom from rhyme and meter. Not only did he find self-expression in the act of poetic expression; the form itself was expressive. This meant more than Pope's dictum: "The sound must seem an echo to the sense"; in many cases the sound (words said aloud) plus connotation *is* the sense, and is always an integral part of it. All poets occasionally use onomatopoeia, but with Whitman the creation of his poem by imitative sound, imitative or symbolical rhythm, and often even "expressive" syntax was the warp and woof of his poetic texture.

This statement needs considerable detailed exemplification to show its importance, and it will be both illustrated and explained throughout the remainder of this chapter, but a couple of examples may serve as preliminary illustrations. The "bridegroom-night of love" passage quoted in Chapter II contains the essentials of Whitman's expressive form: every word in the passage conveys the sensations of the "night of love": "prostrate," "undulating," "clasping," etc., in the "sweet-fleshed" connotations and rhythms of Eros. A more elaborate example is the "oceanic sentence" at the beginning of "Out of the Cradle Endlessly Rocking"—twenty-two lines, in which the subject ("I") is not stated until line 20 and the inverted predicate and object ("a reminiscence sing") not until line 22. All of these structural details convey the subjective meanings of the poem, and with the punctuation, including "psychic rhyme" (repeated words or phrases at the beginning of the lines), combine and co-operate to create space-empathy, kinetic-empathy (such as the feeling of walking on uneven ground), and more complex emotional responses in the reader. These are, perhaps, exceptionally effective examples of expressive form, but the principle holds for *Leaves of Grass* as a whole. It should be noted also that, although Whitman does not in these examples use conventional rhyme and meter, he does use variable patterns of sound created by means of alliteration and assonance, repetition of words and phrases, and rhetorical devices that control the pitch and tone of the voice when the words are recited.

2

Whitman did not suddenly abandon rhyme and meter and begin writing in the prosodic form of "Song of Myself." He retained through all editions of *Leaves of Grass* two poems which show his transition from conventional versification to his new medium of expression. The earlier of these is "Europe," first published on June 21, 1850, in the New York *Daily Tribune* as "Resurgemus," a poetic comment on the year of revolution in Europe, 1848, when revolt failed in France but was successful in Austria and Hungary, and less so in other countries. These events stirred Whitman with the same kind of emotions Whittier had expressed so effectively in rhyme and meter in his Abolition poems.

"Europe" begins with a strongly accented syllable, and the first line scans as "falling rhythm" (*i.e.*, dactylic-trochaic meter), but then shifts to a slightly irregular "rising rhythm" (iambic-anapestic) in the second line, and settles into a definite rising rhythm in the third line.

> Suddenly / out of its / stale and / drowsy / lair, the /
>   lair of / slaves,
> Like lightning it le'pt forth half startled at itself,
> Its feet upon the ashes and the rags, its hands tight
>   to the throats of kings.

Stanza 5 begins with swift-moving anapests, but slows after the caesura in the second line and acquires weight with the heavy emphasis on the occupation substantives:

> But the sweet / ness of merc / y brew'd bit / ter destruc- /
>   tion, and the fright /en'd mon / archs come back,
> Each comes in state with his train, hangman, priest,
>   tax-gatherer,
> Soldier, lawyer, lord, jailer, and sycophant.

Whitman continues to use metrical rhythms (though mixed) throughout the poem, but he varies the meter to suit the thought and emotion, and nowhere better than in the seventh stanza:

> Meanwhile corpses lie in new-made graves, bloody
>   corpses of young men,
> The rope of the gibbet hangs heavily, the bullets of
>   princes are flying, the creatures of power laugh aloud,
> And all these things bear fruits, and they are good.

Not all readers would place equal stress on "all these things bear fruits," but the thought demands slow, emphatic enunciation of the monosyllables. Yet underneath this stress of emotion the metrical feet disintegrate, as in the blank verse of the post-Shakespearean dramatists who influenced T. S. Eliot in his early metrical experiments. We even find rhetorical patterns overshadowing the metrical pattern:

> Those corpses . . . ,
> Those martyrs . . . , those hearts
>
> . . . . .
>
> They live . . . !
> They live . . . ,
> They were purified by death, they were taught and exalted.
>
> Not a grave of the murder'd for freedom but grows seed
>   for freedom, in its turn to bear seed,
> Which the winds carry afar and re-sow, and the rains
>   and the snows nourish.
>
> Not a disembodied spirit can the weapons of tyrants let loose,
> But it stalks invisibly over the earth, whispering, counseling,
>   cautioning.
>
> Liberty, let others despair of you—I never despair of you.
>
> Is the house shut? is the master away?
> Nevertheless, be ready, be not weary of watching,
> He will soon return, his messengers come anon.

By the end of the poem, Whitman has almost found the clausal structure (each verse a sentence, though sometimes elliptical) which he was to use throughout most of *Leaves of Grass*. But before going into "clausal prosody," we might look quickly at the second poem showing Whitman's transition from meter to his own rhythms. It is "A Boston Ballad," almost

certainly written after Whitman had gained command of his
new verse technique, for the event which provoked this satire in
verse (one of the few in *Leaves of Grass*) was the arrest of the
fugitive slave, Anthony Burns, in Boston in June 1854.

Whitman did not retain vestiges of meter in this poem out
of habit or laziness but because he could use them to under-
score his irony. He calls the poem a "ballad," and refers to
"Yankee Doodle Dandy." Fifes and drums shrill and pound
and scream the irony:

> To get / betimes / in Bos / ton town / I rose / this
>   morn / ing early,
>
>   .   .   .   .   .
>
> I love / to look / on the Stars / and Stripes, / I hope /
>   the fifes / will play / Yankee / Doodle.

This merry tune continues through the poet's satirical impera-
tives to the "orderly citizens," whom he commands to exhume
King George III and crown "old buster," because he has
reversed the outcome of the American Revolution.

> Now call for the President's marshal again, bring out
>   the government cannon,
> Fetch home the roarers from Congress, make another procession,
>   guard it with foot and dragoons.
>
> This centre-piece for them;
> Look, all orderly citizens—look from the windows, women!
> The committee open the box, set up the regal ribs, glue
>   those that will not stay,
> Clap the skull on top of the ribs, and clap a crown
>   on top of the skull.

You have got your revenge, old buster—the crown is come
   to its own, and more than its own.
Stick your hands in your pockets, Jonathan—you are a made
   man from this day,
You are mighty cute—and here is one of your bargains.

In the sarcastic emphases of the final couplet the metrical feet lose their identity and the poet's scathing prose voice indicts the moral hypocrisy of "Boston town."

3

The basis of all rhythm is repetition, but there are many kinds of repetition. In metrical verse written in English it is repetition of tonic stresses (or accented syllables) at patterned intervals, but this was not true of older poetry in other countries. For example, early Latin, Old French, and Provençal verse used assonance, the repetition of vowel sounds (without the same preceding and following consonant sounds as in rhyme) to mark the end of verses. Early Germanic and Anglo-Saxon verse used alliteration, repetition of initial consonant sounds, within the verse to mark stresses and give emphasis within a traditional pattern, as in this old Anglo-Saxon gnomic verse:

Wyrd byth swithost. Winter byth cealdost.
(Wyrd [fate] is strongest. Winter is coldest.)

Although assonance has never been a prosodic convention in English verse, and alliteration not since the fourteenth century, both have survived in English and American poetry as decorations or stylistic embellishments, alliteration especially. Whitman made frequent though unsystematic use of both. In lines previously quoted (Chapter III), the alliteration (*p* and *r* sounds) contributes both to the rhythm and to the meaning, and the shifting sounds of *a* and *i* (not true assonance) create tone color, or a kind of word-music:

> Parting tracked by arriving, perpetual payment of
>   the perpetual loan,
> Rich showering rain, and recompense richer afterward.

For a more subtle blending of vowel sounds and alliteration, with connotations simultaneously of soaring and absorbing:

> I fly the flight of the fluid and swallowing soul,
> My course runs below the soundings of plumets.

In using these vestiges of obsolete prosodic methods, Whitman was in no way different from his British contemporaries, Swinburne, Tennyson, the Brownings, and Hopkins, or his countrymen Longfellow and Lowell, but at times he depended upon these conventions more than they did because he had to create his rhythms without the support of a metrical system. Also, after his great lyrical energy began to decline, he fell back more and more upon these older substitutes for meter in his rhythmical improvisations.

But Whitman did have a prosodic system—or at least a general practice, for he never consciously reduced it to a system. This practice was a *clausal prosody*, or *thought rhythm*, based on patterns of statements: his verse-unit was not the metrical foot of conventional prosody or the phrase of *vers libre* but the statement, usually an independent clause. In a series of parallel statements he could create a rhythm not only of thought but also of sounds, because the repetition of thought is often achieved by repetition of words and hence sounds. This clausal-principle can be emphasized by spacing his verses as if the parallels were rhymes:

> I celebrate myself,
> and sing myself,
>> And what I assume
>> you shall assume,
>>> For every atom belonging to me
>>> as good belongs to you.

> I loafe and invite my soul,
> I lean and loafe at my ease observing a spear
>> of summer grass.
> My tongue, every atom of my blood, form'd from
>> this soil, this air,
> Born here of parents born here from parents the
>> same, and their parents the same,
>>> I, now thirty-seven years old in perfect health begin,
>>> Hoping to cease not till death.

This use of parallelism as a structural and rhythmical principle closely resembles the prosody of Biblical poetry, which scholars[9] have often thought to have been Whitman's source, as it could well have been, because he was thoroughly familiar with the King James Bible.[10] But he may not have consciously molded his new prosody on any analogies. He could have evolved his technique simply by experimentation and improvisation in his search for rhythmical ways of expressing what he was trying to "sing" or "chant." The poetry of almost all primitive peoples and of the early civilizations has similar rhythmical structures based on parallelisms and reiterations found in *Leaves of Grass*. In 1898 Pasquale Jannaccone pointed this out in his *La Poesia di Walt Whitman e L'Evoluzione delle Forme Ritmiche*, beginning with Hebraic examples in the Latin Vulgate:

> benedicit tibi benedictionibus coeli desuper
> benedictionibus abyssi jacentis deorsum
> benedictionibus uberum et vulvae.[11]

> ([The Almighty] who shall bless thee with blessings of
> heaven above, blessings of the deep that lieth under,
> blessings of the breasts, and of the womb.)   Genesis 49:25

> Dixit Balaam filius Beor,
> Dixit homo cui obturatus est oculus,
> Dixit auditor sermonum dei.

> (Balaam the son of Beor hath said, and the man whose eyes are open hath said: He hath said, which heard the words of God.)   Numbers 24:3-4

"But the examples which have the closest affinity to Whitman's lyricism," says Jannaccone, "are those in Greek syntonic prose of patristic literature."[12] He then cites several passages from St. Sophronius's homily on Mary's Annunciation, among them these lines:

> ᾔδει γὰρ, ἐχ τούτου θεογνωσία τὸν χόσμον
>   αὐγάζεσθαι·
> ᾔδει, τῆς πλανης τὴν ἀχλὺν ἀφανίζεσθαι·
> ᾔδει, τοῦ θανάτου το χέντρον
>   ἀμβλύνεσθαι.[13]

(Thus she was learning thereby of the illumining of the world
  with the knowledge of God;
She was learning of the vanishing of error's gloom;
She was learning of the dulling of death's sting.)

Similar examples of verses with parallel thoughts and repeated words or phrases can be found in translations of North American Indian songs, chants of the aborigines of Australia, of the pygmies of Africa, and of other peoples without a written language—see C. M. Bowra's *Primitive Song* (1962). None of these Whitman is likely to have known, and their only significance in relation to his verse is that they show how nearly he had come to recovering (subjectively or intuitively) some of the earliest poetic techniques of mankind. If he could have known this, he would doubtless have been greatly pleased, because in his poems he was striving to recover the prelapsarian innocence and potency of Adam—to "ascend," as he says at the beginning of the "Children of Adam" poems, to the Garden of Eden.

Finding analogies between Whitman's verse techniques and those of genuine "primitive song" can, however, be misleading, for the primitive verse is usually extremely monotonous with its tom-tom reiterations just for the sake of the sound and rhythm, like the Arapaho song of the Peyote cult quoted by Bowra:[14]

ye no wi ci hay
yo wi hay
wi ci hay
yo wi ci no
wi ci ni

These nonsense sounds are repeated over and over again. In an

Eskimo weather incantation intelligible words are used, but they are only:

> Clouds, clouds,
> Clouds, clouds down below,
> Clouds, clouds,
> Clouds, clouds down below.[15]

Whitman also at times seems to be engaging in incantation but his emotions are more often comparable to those of the Hebraic poets in their praise and adoration of their Deity. Whitman, of course, is not so much in love with God as with His Creation, which he adores even in his adoration of himself. Though the form of the litany in Psalm 70 is different from Whitman's nature paeans, it has precisely the pattern of repetition used in most of the strophes or verse-clusters in *Leaves of Grass*:

> Make haste, O God, to deliver me;
> Make haste to help me, O Lord.
>
> Let them be ashamed and confounded that seek after my soul;
> Let them be turned backward and brought to dishonour
>   that delight in my hurt.
> Let them be turned back by reason of their shame that
>   say Aha, Aha.
> Let all those that seek thee rejoice and be glad in thee;
> And let such as love thy salvation say continually
>
>   Let God be magnified.
>
> But I am poor and needy; make haste unto me, O God!
> Thou art my help and my deliverer; O Lord, make no tarrying.[16]

This prayer is in the form of an envelope, beginning with the plea to God to "make haste," then the enumeration of wished-for events, and the repeated plea to "make no tarrying." Whitman seldom used the envelope, but the general pattern of statement and enumeration, repeated statement and enumeration, is his most frequent pattern. A typical example, sung not with the aggressive humility of the Hebraic poet but with wonder and delight that nature and life—and death—are as they are, is section 6 of "Song of Myself," with its beautiful adoration of the grass:

And now it seems to me the beautiful uncut hair of graves.

Tenderly will I use you curling grass,
It may be you transpire from the breasts of young men,
It may be if I had known them I would have loved them,
It may be you are from old people, or from offspring
    taken soon out of their mothers' laps,
And here you are the mother's laps.

This grass is very dark to be from the white heads of
    old mothers,
Darker than the colorless beards of old men,
Dark to come from under the faint red roofs of mouths.

O I perceive after all so many uttering tongues,
And I perceive they do not come from the roofs of
    mouths for nothing.

I wish I could translate the hints about the dead young
    men and women,
And the hints about old men and mothers, and the offspring
    taken soon out of their laps.

What do you think has become of the young and old men?
And what do you think has become of the women and children?

They are alive and well somewhere,
The smallest sprout shows there is really no death.
And if ever there was it led forward life, and does not
    wait at the end to arrest it,
And ceas'd the moment life appear'd.

All goes forward and outward, nothing collapses,
And to die is different from what any one supposed, and luckier.

But for an example of more Biblical cadences—and the same
techniques of repeating words and phrases—consider "Song of
the Answerer." A young man comes to the poet with a message
from his brother asking for "signs" by which he may recognize
the poet-messiah:

And I stand before the young man face to face, and take his
    right hand in my left hand and his left hand in my
    right hand,
And I answer for his brother and for men, and I answer for
    him that answers for all, and send these signs.

Him all wait for, him all yield up to, his word is decisive
    and final,
Him they accept, in him lave, in him perceive themselves
    as amid light,
Him they immerse and he immerses them.
                . . . . .
He is the Answerer,
What can be answer'd he answers, and what cannot be
    answer'd he shows how it cannot be answer'd.

This incremental repetition is not only stylized but even ritualized: right hand in left hand, left hand in right hand; him—him; answer—answer'd, etc. Few poems in *Leaves of Grass* so definitely echo the ritual language of Hebraic poetry, but it is significant that a modern Israeli poet has remarked that *Leaves of Grass* in Hebrew sounded to him like Ezekiel.[17]

4

In his most successful lyrical passages Whitman combines patterns of tonic stress with subtle musical effects in his variations of time patterns and parallelism of thought, grammatical structure, and word reiteration. A virtuoso example is the symbolical love-making in section 21 of "Song of Myself." To intensify the erotic connotations, the poet personifies night and describes her (?) approach to earth as if he were describing Jove descending from the sky—a super-human point of view (before the age of cosmonauts), but the love-relationship is humanized by the poet's emotional identification with both "night" and "earth." As he "walks" with night, he feels her erotic attraction and calls out the imagined earth's desire for closer contact:

> I am he that walks with the tender and growing night,
> I call to the earth and sea half-held by the night.
>
> Press close bare-bosom'd night—press close magnetic nourishing night!
> Night of south winds—night of the large few stars!
> Still nodding night—mad naked summer night.
>
> Smile O voluptuous cool-breath'd earth!
> Earth of the slumbering and liquid trees!

Earth of the departed sunset—earth of the mountains misty-topt!
Earth of the vitreous pour of the full moon just tinged with
  blue!
Earth of shine and dark mottling the tide of the river!
Earth of the limpid gray of clouds brighter and clearer for my
  sake!
Far-swooping elbow'd earth—rich-apple blossom'd earth!
Smile, for your lover comes.

Prodigal, you have given me love—therefore I to you give love!
O unspeakable passionate love!

The introductory couplet in this passage is almost metrical
with the rhythm of walking "with the tender and growing
night." The voyeur's rapture becomes so strong that the rhythm
is almost monopodic:

  Press close bare-bosom'd night—

Then the cadence is varied by the addition of unstressed
syllables:

  . . . press close magnetic nourishing night!

The subtle variations in accentuation and timing continue in
the following lines—and indeed throughout the poem:

  Night of south winds—night of the large few stars!

The difference between "few large stars" and the unexpected
"large few stars" is the difference between trite sound and sense
and a phrase with highly connotative rhythm and emphasis.
The vocalic *lä* merging into the vibrant *rg* sound intensifies not

only the adjective "large" but the whole phrase, making it stand out like the "few stars" in the night sky. The fourth stress in the second half of the following line also adds weight and *largo* effect:

Stíll nódding níght—mad náked súmmer níght.

The blending of cosmic spaciousness and human dimensions in the imagery also harmonizes with the shortening and lengthening of the cadences. The feminine night is "tender," "bare-bosom'd," "nodding" (ready for bed?), and "naked." The earth is "voluptuous" and "cool-breath'd"; though "far-sweeping" in his (?) circuit around the sun, the elliptical orbit is compared to the bend of a human elbow. Out of context, these metaphors sound naïvely sentimental, but in the total context of Whitman's expressive form they convey the sensuous encounter of night, earth, and the observing poet, who in his fantasy is as "prodigal" (liberal) in love, giving and receiving, as "tender" night and "voluptuous" earth.

However, section 21 is not unique in having its own expressive rhythms and diction, for each of the fifty-two sections has its appropriate shape and form. "Song of Myself" is not, as previously asserted by various critics (including myself), a mosaic.[18] Often a single section could stand alone as a self-contained poem, but read in sequence the sections give a progression of thought, symbols, and emotional intensity up to the final word in the poem—"boot-soles." As indicated in Chapter IV, the protagonist "I" is searching for the meaning of self in the cycle of birth, death, and rebirth: a search that begins with "observing a spear of summer grass" (5) and continues across the face of the continent, soars into space (terrestial and celestial) and through time—"the caresser of life wherever moving, backward as well as forward sluing" (232); extending from the beginning of the "huge first Nothing" (1153) through history (sec. 34–35), through death (sec. 49–50), finally returning to the grass, there to wait for the reader.

The form and structure vary not only with each section, but even in the strophes (the grouped lines) within the sections. In section 26 the poet announces: "Now I will do nothing but listen," and then enumerates in parallel statements what he hears, until seventeen lines later he approaches an emotional climax in hearing "a grand opera":

> A tenor large and fresh as the creation fills me,
> The orbic flex of his mouth is pouring and filling me full.
>
> I hear the train'd soprano (what work with hers is this?)
> The orchestra whirls me wider than Uranus flies,
> It wrenches such ardors from me I did not know I possess'd
>   them,
> It sails me, I dab with bare feet, they are lick'd by the
>   indolent waves,
> I am cut by bitter and angry hail, I lose my breath,
> Steep'd amid honey'd morphine, my windpipe throttled in
>   fakes of death,
> At length let up again to feel the puzzle of puzzles,
> And that we call Being.

After the near-faint in the paroxysm of ecstasy, the rhythm returns to repose, control, with the finality of clashed cymbals at the end of a symphony: "And *that* we call *Be-ing*."

The motif of section 33 is vision—and motion, because change of observation point is necessary for seeing a great diversity of objects and places. Many lines begin with the adverb of place:

Where the panther walks to and fro on a limb overhead,
  where the buck turns furiously at the hunter,
Where the rattlesnake suns his flabby length on a rock,
  where the otter is feeding on fish,
Where the alligator in his tough pimples sleeps by the bayou,
Where the black bear is searching for roots or honey, where
  the beaver pats the mud with his paddle-shaped tail . . .

These long lines filled with enumerations—"catalogues" they
have been called derisively—are means by which the poet
"incarnates" the life and scenes of his country. And they are
more than catalogues, accumulations, for each image is sharply
focused: "geese nip their food with short jerks . . . wolves bark
amid wastes of snow and icicled trees . . . the katy-did works her
chromatic reed on the walnut-tree over the well . . ."

The tempo changes with the fantasy of "speeding through
space"—with Saturn, the moon, and "tail'd meteors, throwing
fire-balls like the rest"—and slows again as the protagonist
returns to earth and identifies with men and women in mar-
riage, sickness, death, martyrdom, and warfare. Sections 34–35
detail specific historical events, and 37 the pathetic scenes of
prison, pestilence, and beggary. Then this moody tone and
tempo are broken in section 38—suddenly, violently:

Enough! enough! enough!
Somehow I have been stunn'd. Stand back!

But he recovers from his shock, remembers his mission, resumes
"the overstaid fraction" of his life, and troops "forth replen-
ish'd with supreme power, one in an average unending procession." By section 40 the protagonist's confidence has become so
sure that he tells the sunshine jauntily to "lie over" and make

room for him, and calls the earth sarcastically "old top knot." (Here the "American humor" which Chase finds is unmistakably evident.) As the leader of a new religion in section 41, he resumes the prophetic tone, but exclaims with a mixture of arrogance and self-mockery: "By my life-lumps! becoming already a creator"; then announces sententiously the birth of his religious role: "Putting myself here and now to the ambush'd womb of the shadows." In this role he calls to the crowd (sec. 42), "Come my children," and begins his virtuoso oration, by turns soothing, exclamatory, sarcastic, and prayerful (49):

> And as to you Death, and you bitter hug of mortality,
>   it is idle to try to alarm me.
>
>   . . . .
>
> I hear you whispering there O stars of heaven,
> O suns—O grass of graves—O perpetual transfers and promo-
>   tions . . .

In the following section (50) the rhythms as well as the words carry the burden of the sermon on the meaning of *death* in the new religion:

> Wrench'd and sweaty—calm and cool then my body becomes,
> I sleep—I sleep long.
>
> I do not know it—it is without name—it is a word unsaid,
> It is not in any dictionary, utterance, symbol.
>
> Something it swings on more than the earth swings on,
> To it the creation is the friend whose embracing awakes me.
>
> Do you see O my brothers and sisters?

It is not chaos or death—it is form, union, plan
  it is eternal life—it is Happiness.

The word order is inverted for rhythm as well as emphasis of thought:

Wrench'd and sweaty—
calm and cool
then my body becomes,
I sleep—
I sleep long.

Shifting to a confiding tone of voice, the speaker says calmly but with deep fervor, "I do not know it . . . Perhaps I might tell more . . ."; then like an evangelical preacher shouts "Outlines!" and resumes with even voice but firm conviction.

The sermon ends in section 51, and in 52 the speaker, accused by the "spotted hawk" of longwindedness, gives his conclusion in succinct couplet and triplet parallelism, with an effect something like that of a coda at the end of a symphony. The rising rhythm is quickened by the use of unstressed syllables:

I depart as air, I shake my white locks at the runaway sun,
I effuse my flesh in eddies, and drift it in lacy jags.

And in the same tone, with mixed anapests and iambs:

I bequeath / myself / to the dirt / to grow / from the
  grass / I love

This is a lovely, rippling verse, in slightly elevated language (*e.g.*, "bequeath"); but without a noticeable shift in rhythm and diction the following line becomes colloquial and the verse sounds more like prose:

If you want me again look for me under your boot-soles.

Then a triplet which could be read as prose except for the metrical third line:

You will hardly know who I am or what I mean,
But I shall be good health to you nevertheless,
And filter and fiber your blood.

The final triplet is also in measured accents, low-keyed, but memorable for the simplicity of diction and emphasis which persuasively encourages "you" to expect and search for the buried poet-prophet (or protagonist-self):

Failing to fetch me at first keep encouraged,
Missing me one place search another,
I stop somewhere waiting for you.

Thus the poem is, finally, mythic—Frazer's "buried God" motif—and imagery, rhythms, and rhetoric combine to symbolize a *resurrected self*, purified by death.

5

"The Sleepers" was also one of the twelve untitled poems of the first edition, and the erotic imagery of the first version is more interesting for a psychological study of the poet and his art than any of the later versions, but for aesthetic analysis the final text serves well enough. That Whitman himself was of several minds about the poem is indicated by his changing the title from "Night Poem" (1856), "Sleep-Chasings" (1860), to "The Sleepers" (1871–92). Malcolm Cowley calls it "a fantasia of the unconscious,"[19] a more concise way of saying what Dr. R. M. Bucke, Whitman's first biographer, had attempted in 1883 when he called it "a representation of the mind during sleep—of connected, half-connected, and disconnected thoughts and feelings as they occur in dreams . . ."[20] One probable difference in the intentions of these two commentators is that Cowley very likely meant that Whitman quite literally tapped his unconscious (as in sleep) while composing the poem. Though Dr. Bucke believed that Whitman experienced "cosmic consciousness"[21] (mystical intuitions of divine or cosmic truth), "representation" implies the artistic imitation or dramatization of dreams.

Edwin Miller calls the poem "Whitman's most personal revelation" of his sexual psychology, and a re-enactment of ancient puberty rites.

> Unlike a dream, the poem does not end inconclusively, but as in a rite of adolescence the protagonist experiences the terrors of anticipated initiation, with its physical pain, as well as the attendant joys of entrance into manhood and into society— except that the drama of Whitman's poem, of necessity, is played out in the protagonist's consciousness, and that the conclusion is sublimation.[22]

In this interpretation the episodes of defeat and terror in sections 3–6 symbolize the poet's fear of pain; the happy images that follow in sections 7–8 symbolize the "joys of entrance into manhood." But a more direct and less hypothetical interpretation is simply that sleep and night in the poem symbolize death, regeneration, and rebirth.

"The Sleepers" is capable of these different interpretations because of the manner in which the poet employs his symbols. In prosodic form and thematic structure the poem resembles "Song of Myself," but the theme of wandering "all night in my vision" gives it a more compact and unified order, with the obvious Aristotelian beginning, middle, and end ("Song of Myself" has these, but they are far from obvious). Furthermore, the identification and metamorphoses techniques of "Song of Myself" are quite natural for the poet of "The Sleepers," for everyone has experienced such transformations in his dreams. Whitman showed himself to have been an acute observer of his own dream psychology—and he had also read Swedenborg.[23] But the structure of the poem shows a considerable degree of conscious planning and control of its contents.

At the very beginning the protagonist is more than an abstraction, or mere literary device:

> I wander all night in my vision,
> Stepping with light feet, swiftly and noiselessly
>   stepping and stopping,
> Bending with open eyes over the shut eyes of sleepers,
> Wandering and confused, lost to myself, ill-assorted,
>   contradictory,
> Pausing, gazing, bending, and stopping.

The fourth line indicates that this is more than an imaginary dream-flight, or a reminiscence either. In a sleepwalking trance the wandering "I" might be "confused," but the other words imply deeper psychic disturbances. The protagonist, therefore, is searching for an answer to some question or problem that disturbs him. In his search through—and over—the world, he identifies with the other sleepers and dreams their dreams, both of the happy and of the dissatisfied dreamers. Each sleeps and dreams according to his nature and condition. The protagonist sympathizes with "the worst-suffering and the most restless," and calms them by passing his hand "soothingly to and fro a few inches from them." But some of his actions are ambiguous:

Now I pierce the darkness, new beings appear,
The earth recedes from me into the night,
I saw that it was beautiful, and I see that what is
    not the earth is beautiful.

The protagonist in "Song of Myself" soared into space, afoot with his vision, but here, who are the "new beings"? Are they physical creatures or spirits? Probably they are spirits, "what is not the earth," and again Swedenborg may be the source of the fantasy, for he traveled back and forth between the two worlds. At any rate, what the protagonist has seen is so exhilarating that he feels himself to be a dance—not a dancer, but the activity—and the music he calls for is evidently divine. He himself, "the ever-laughing," becomes godlike in his ability to see "nimble ghosts" and spy out concealed treasures, even if hidden deep in the ground or sea. Hiding "douceurs" is esoteric (unless a misunderstood French word), but he does find sweetness and fragrances everywhere, placed there apparently by the "journeymen divine," who become his willing servants. He leads them in bacchanalian joy. Then he resumes, like Bacchus (Dionysius), his metamorphoses and plays various roles, including the lonely woman pining for a lover, whom she receives in the guise of darkness. He becomes a grandmother, a widow, and a shroud wrapped around a corpse in the grave. This makes him feel that all living things ought to be happy just for the privilege of being alive.

Sections 3–6 are episodic: the beautiful naked swimmer

killed by the waves, a shipwreck (reminiscent of Margaret Full-er's fate off Fire Island, Long Island), the battle at Brooklyn in which General Washington was defeated. The episodes are all of defeats, including the idyll of the "red squaw" who visited the poet's mother and then disappeared, never to return. But these pathetic visions give way to fulfillments of desire for beauty, safety, and love. The suffering, the criminal, the wronged, the idiot, are cured and restored by "night and sleep," which wash away their degradation and pain and "average" them.

> I swear they are all beautiful,
> Every one that sleeps is beautiful, every thing in the
>   dim light is beautiful,
> The wildest and bloodiest is over, and all is peace.
>
> Peace is always beautiful,
> The myth of heaven indicates peace and night.

Symbolical "sleep" and "night" at this point in the allegory are capable of several interpretations, not altogether unrelated.

> The myth of heaven indicates the soul,
> The soul is always beautiful, it appears more or it
>   appears less, it comes or it lags behind,
> It comes from its embower'd garden and looks pleasantly
>   on itself and encloses the world,
> Perfect and clean the genitals previously jetting, and
>   perfect and clean the womb cohering,
> The head well-grown proportion'd and plumb, and the
>   bowels and joints proportion'd and plumb.

Though "The soul is always beautiful," the body in which it is housed may not be, such as the "twisted skull," the child deformed by venereal parents or drunken ones; but the soul will not be contaminated by these accidents and will eventually find rebirth in a beautiful body:

> The sleepers that lived and died wait, the far advanced are
>   to go on in their turns, and the far behind are to
>   come on in their turns,
> The diverse shall be no less diverse, but they shall flow
>   and unite—they unite now.

Through death ("sleep") the soul is released from earthly imperfections, and all become equally beautiful and happy in a realm of absolute love. Nietzsche would say this is "wishful thinking,"[24] or Freud the desire to return to the womb, and Whitman calls it the "myth of heaven." Nevertheless, the final dream of the protagonist of this poem is that

> The sleepers are very beautiful as they lie unclothed,
> They flow hand in hand over the whole earth from east to west
>   as they lie unclothed,
>
>   . . . . .
>
> They pass the invigoration of the night and the chemistry
>   of the night, and awake.

The healing, restoring sleep is more than death, releasing the soul from the encumbering body; it is not, after all, the Christian myth of heaven, but a myth of rebirth, with some resemblance to the Hindu reincarnation.

> I too pass from the night,
> I stay a while away O night, but I return to you again and
>   love you.

Why should I be afraid to trust myself to you?
I am not afraid, I have been well brought forward by you,
I love the rich running day, but I do not desert her in
    whom I lay so long,
I know not how I came of you and I know not where I go with
    you,
. . . . but I know I came well and shall go well.

In the physical life he stays away from night (death-mother-realm of soul), but he will return and become one among all the other beautiful sleepers. He has learned, however, not only to love night-death but also to have confidence in day-life, knowing that all the scars acquired during the day will be cured and erased on his return to mother-night:

I will stop only a time with the night, and rise betimes,
I will duly pass the day O my mother and duly return to you.

The ritual language and rhythms of this ending give the poem the overtones of religious revelation and prophecy, and the image of the sleepers flowing hand in hand over the whole world might be one of William Blake's symbolical drawings.

6

With "Crossing Brooklyn Ferry" (first published in 1856 as "Sun-Down Poem"), Whitman began not a new form but a more organized structure of his poems. Although this poem is neither a description nor a narration of a physical trip across the East River to Manhattan, the motif of such a trip (like Thoreau's "week" on the two rivers) gives the poet the real subject of his poem, which is his meditations on defying time by preserving his transitory experiences in art—the theme of some of Shakespeare's sonnets and of Keats's "Ode on a Grecian Urn." But, except for the theme, Whitman's poem in no way resembles any of Shakespeare's sonnets or Keats's "Ode"; and the difference is in the form, structure, and diction.

"Crossing Brooklyn Ferry" begins in reminiscence—the historical present:

> Flood-tide below me! I see you face to face!
> Clouds of the west—sun there half an hour high—
>   I see you face to face.
>
> Crowds of men and women attired in the usual costumes,
>   how curious you are to me!
> On the ferry-boats the hundreds and hundreds that cross,
>   returning home, are more curious to me than you suppose,
> And you that shall cross from shore to shore years hence are
>   more curious to me, and more in my meditations, than
>   you might suppose.

As the poet invokes the memory of the river at flood tide half an hour before sunset (a symbol of death), he feels himself to be again one of the crowd on the ferry and projects the memory backward and forward in time, both reliving and anticipating his experience as an integral part in the unity of boat, tide, crowd, and the two shores; and he can easily imagine an endless repetition of the experience. Ergo, by preserving the memory in a poem that will continue to be read long after his death, he will have caused time to stand still, or cease to exist. His creative problem is finding images, rhythms, and grammatical structures to *express* this paradox of stasis in motion. He succeeds not by the use of new prosodic or linguistic techniques but in adapting those of "Song of Myself." At a glance, the poem is seen to have the same strophe units based on a group of parallel statements (ending with a period), the same use of a

repeated word or phrase at the beginning of the line. And variation of the rhythms is achieved by shifting accentual patterns.
But these are subtly adapted to the theme and tone of the ferry
allegory—for it is an allegory of life and art, or life turned into
art.

The poem contains little if any imitative rhythm. No
attempt is made to simulate the throb of the engine propelling
the ferry, or the motion of the boat, the flow of the tide
(though the imagery conveys its flow), or the vocal sounds of
the passengers. These may be felt (or imagined) by the reader,
but they are evoked by the order and connotations of the words
and images rather than by manipulated patterns of tone and
volume or tempo of sounds. Section 1 simply images the flood
tide and crowds of men and women on ferryboats—not of one
boat or a particular trip, but the essence of many trips. Section 2 has two strophes, or sentence-paragraphs. The first merely
states representative details (images) of the scene in which the
poet feels himself to be both in and out of the game of the
"well-join'd scheme"—the unity during the interval aboard the
ferry of water, boat, people, etc.:

> The impalpable sustenance of me from all things at all
>   hours of the day,
> The simple, compact, well-join'd scheme, myself disintegrated,
>   everyone disintegrated yet part of the scheme,
> The similitudes of the past and those of the future,
> The glories strung like beads on my smallest sights and hearings,
>   on the walk in the street and the passage over the river,
> The current rushing so swiftly and swimming with me far away,
> The others that are to follow me, the ties between me and
>   them,
> The certainty of others, the life, love, sight, hearing of
>   others.

Some of these lines are independent clauses (all independent if ellipses of predicates are recognized), but the whole strophe implies rather than states the predication: These are what I *have* experienced. The second strophe states more explicitly that others "are to follow me," a merging of present and future, forming a tie between "me" and them. The second strophe uses *will* and predicts what others will see; but though more specific details are enumerated than in the previous strophe, they are details which the poet *has seen.*

Having no narration, section 2 does not progress in time or place, but the succession of images—ferry gates, flowing tide, shores, ships, Brooklyn Heights, the sun low on the horizon, etc.—give an illusion of motion. Though the time of the poem is half an hour before sunset, the day and the clock-hour are irrelevant because in section 3 the season is both winter ("Twelfth-month") and summer; it is no-time and all-time, which is the theme of the section. "It avails not, time nor place—distance avails not . . . " This paradox is symbolized in sky and water, in the circling gulls, "high in the air, floating with motionless wings, oscillating their bodies,"

> Saw the slow-wheeling circles and the gradual edging
>   toward the south,
> Saw the reflection of the summer sky in the water,
> Had my eyes dazzled by the shimmering track of beams,
> Look'd at the fine centrifugal spokes of light round
>   the shape of my head in the sunlit water . . .

The movement of the poem is centrifugal. The trip is from portal to portal, and the experiencing "I" sees his own halo in the water, which also ebbs and flows. The passengers, too, who cross over to Manhattan will later return to Brooklyn, perhaps make the round trip many times, as the poet *has* done and *will* do. Life and death are also circular. Individuals emerge from the "float" and return to it.

> I too had been struck from the float forever held in solution,
> I too had receiv'd identity by my body . . .

"Float," a metaphor for the salt water (or ocean) in the East River, is obviously symbolical, whether it be interpreted as the equivalent of Emerson's Over-Soul, Chari's "cosmic consciousness," or Edwin Miller's womb and amniotic fluid. The word is repeated in line 106 as "eternal float of solution" and is invoked to "suspend." In the chemical sense, "solution" means a fluid in which the ingredients remain dissolved and seemingly unified. However, in the context of the poet's invocations to the river to "flow," the waves to "frolic," the clouds to "drench" with their splendor (not *shine* or *radiate* but *drench*, like a soaking rain), the masts and hills to "stand up," the brain to "throb," we would expect the word "suspend" to have a strongly active, positive meaning: such as remain capable of producing new living "identities" to continue the process of birth-out-of-death.

That the poet is calling for more life, more vibrant activity, more sense gratifications, is implied in the succeeding lines in which he commands the "loving and thirsty eyes" to *gaze*, the voices of young men to *sound out* and call him (the poet) by his "nighest name." In the same spirit, he also feels his kinship with common, average humanity, including their weaknesses and perversities. In spite of human faults, all lives have emerged from the "eternal float" and each person who looks into the shimmering water will see "fine spokes of light" haloing his head, just as the poet has. And all these objects which delight the senses are "ministers" to their souls, reminders of the spiritual basis of all existence (the American Transcendental doctrine previously mentioned). Like the child in the poem who went forth every day and every object he looked upon "became part of him for the day . . . Or for many years . . ." the poet now assures these "beautiful ministers":

> We use you, and do not cast you aside—we plant you
>   permanently within us,
> We fathom you not—we love you—there is perfection
>   in you also,
> You furnish your parts toward eternity,
> Great or small, you furnish your parts toward the soul.

Edwin Miller has compared "Crossing Brooklyn Ferry" to Wallace Stevens's "hedonistic statement of faith in his famous "Sunday Morning"—high praise in itself—, but he goes on to say that "Crossing Brooklyn Ferry" is, organically, part of the flux it depicts. In this respect, "it is far more subtly organized than 'Sunday Morning'."[25] In the terms of this chapter, "Crossing Brooklyn Ferry" is one of Whitman's greatest successes in the aesthetic use of expressive form and structure.

7

"Walt Whitman's method in the construction of his songs is strictly the method of the Italian Opera," declared an anonymous reviewer,[26] now believed to have been Whitman himself, in the *Saturday Press* on January 7, 1860, in reply to a vicious attack in a Cincinnati newspaper.[27] In the early 1850s, attending performances of Italian opera was a passionate experience for Whitman[28]—see his own description in a passage quoted on page 176—and the music of the opera may well have influenced his own creations in verbal music. But except in a very loose and figurative way, it is difficult to find the "method" of an operatic work in "Song of Myself," "Crossing Brooklyn Ferry," or, indeed, in any of his poems before "Out of the Cradle Endlessly Rocking." Actually it was this very poem which the Cincinnati critic denounced (then called "A Child's Reminiscence"), and if Whitman's claim is limited to this poem, it may be at least partly granted, for this poem does have operatic "methods" and marks a new phase in the technique of Whitman's poetic art.

"Out of the Cradle Endlessly Rocking" begins with a prologue which rhythmically imitates the rocking movement of the ocean in the first line and echoes it in succeeding lines, which repeat "Out . . . Out of . . . ," and then begins each line with an adverb or a preposition that both in rhythm and in association suggests uneven footing on the sandy beach in the incident the poet recalls from childhood: "Over . . . Down . . . Up from . . . Out from . . . From . . . From . . . From . . . ," etc. The long opening sentence continuing through twenty-two lines has been called "oceanic," and it is both expansive and dactylic, a rhythm which suggests the restless movement of the sea. Whitman also gets part of this rhythmical and emotional effect by beginning the sentences with modifiers and circuitously approaching the predication, which is thus subordinated to the descriptive and tangential details. His story—and for once he has a story to tell—is less important than how it is felt to have happened and what the man-poet remembering the boy-observer now feels that it means. Everything in the poem tends to be simile or metaphor on the way to becoming symbols.

Even the second sentence (lines 23–31) introduces the place, time, objects observed, and at last the subject (observer "I") elliptically and indirectly:

Once Paumanok,
When the lilac-scent was in the air and Fifth-month
   grass was growing,
Up this seashore in some briars,
Two feather'd guests from Alabama, two together,
And their nest, and four light-green eggs spotted with brown,
And every day the he-bird to and fro near at hand,
And every day the she-bird crouch'd on her nest, silent,
   with bright eyes,
And every day I, a curious boy, never too close, never
   disturbing them,
Cautiously peering, absorbing, translating.

The first strophe (or sentence) is lyrical: if not actually sung, it makes more impression as sound than as statement, and it could easily be chanted. The second strophe is not the least prosaic either, but its implied tone is not that of the speaking voice. It corresponds to the recitative, or talking part in opera. But the song of the bird is, naturally, in the form of an aria—the solo part of an opera—with strongly accented patterns of rhythm and repeated words and phrases for the sake of the sound: clear, now loud, now soft, always deeply emotional:

Shine! shine! shine!
Pour down your warmth, great sun!
While we bask, we two together.

Two together!
Winds blow south, or winds blow north,
Day come white, or night come black,
Home, or rivers and mountains from home,
Singing all time, minding no time,
While we two keep together.

The arias of the mockingbird are interspersed with the recitative of the reminiscing poet, who continues the narrative and speaks to the mourning bird, and finally surmises the meaning of the drama he has observed. The song of the bird is rendered subjectively—what the boy-man feels it to mean. The poet makes no attempt to imitate the notes of the mockingbird, with its fantastic repertoire of runs and trills and chirps and liquid flutings, repeated with endless variations. The virtuoso musical performance of the mockingbird is beyond the power of the human voice or language to suggest except in metaphor, and impossible to imitate.

But the sound of the mockingbird's song is not what Whitman is trying to express in these arias, but its subjective implications. The song symbolizes the pathos of death, which all living creatures must suffer. And it is the sea, personified as "the savage old mother" rocking her cradle, which utters the "delicious word death," taken by the poet as consolation. The story of the mockingbird mourning for its lost mate is almost excessively sentimental, but this is not the theme of the poem. What the poem is really about is how the boy became a man and a poet through the childhood initiation into the mystery of death and maternity. The "old crone" rocks the cradle of death, but the function of cradles and mothers is to produce and protect new lives. The promise of rebirth is not stated in the poem, but it is perhaps implied by these symbols, though they have also been interpreted to mean the poet's subconscious wish to return to the safety of the womb, and the imagery, connotations, and rhythms of the final lines do imply the seductiveness of the death-principle:

My own songs awaked from that hour,
And with them the key, the word up from the waves,

The word of the sweetest song and all songs,
That strong and delicious word which, creeping to my feet,
(Or like some old crone rocking the cradle, swathed in
    sweet garments, bending aside,)
The sea whisper'd me.

8

Throughout the Civil War years Whitman wrote poems which he published at the end of the war as *Drum-Taps*. Since most of them are topical, the product of some episode or specific phase of his experience during the war, they are in the main brief, concise, and less ambitious than Whitman's earlier poems. Before printing the book, he wrote his friend William O'Connor that he thought it would be "superior to *Leaves of Grass*—certainly more perfect as a work of art," adding, "*Drum-Taps* has none of the perturbations of *Leaves of Grass*." By "perturbations" he evidently meant emotional turmoils which either motivated or in some way affected his writing of poems before the war—probably the "Calamus" poems especially. This opinion is only important in the present context because it indicates that Whitman was deliberately striving for artistry, and the poems themselves show the effort. Actually they are not aesthetically superior to Whitman's earlier poems but for the most part are more conventional, less boldly imaginative, and less characteristic of his poetry as a whole. Perhaps the strain of his experiences in the military hospitals drained away his creative energy, or it may have been declining anyway—for some of the unimpressive poems in *Drum-Taps* were written before Whitman left Brooklyn for Washington. The important fact, however, is that in the early 1860s Whitman was gradually modifying the poetic techniques which he had used so brilliantly in "Song of Myself," "The Sleepers," "Crossing Brooklyn Ferry," and "Out of the Cradle Endlessly Rocking."

The "Drum-Taps" collection begins with a "Prelude" in which Whitman praises Manhattan for its prompt and loyal support of the Union cause. The label marks this as a "set-piece." But the poem "Beat! Beat! Drums!" at least has the mad enthusiasm of the patriot, and its crude tom-tom rhythm is appropriate for its function as a recruiting poem. However, in too many of the poems the symbolism and the personifications are stereotyped, as in:

> From Paumanok starting I fly like a bird,
> Around and around to soar to sing the idea of all.

Even though the earlier "Starting from Paumanok" was a "program-poem," the poet did not try "to soar to sing the idea of all." The longer poem called "Song of the Banner at Daybreak" has even more flabby language and threadbare symbolism, with its preaching flag and catechism between the child, the father, and the poet. "Rise O Days from Your Fathomless Deep" is less trite in language, but also has obvious personifications of abstractions.

However, in between the prelude and an epilogue about the soil "leaven'd" with the blood of heroes, there are some vivid vignettes of "Cavalry Crossing a Ford"; a very pathetic "Come up from the Fields Father," which authentically re-enacts the common drama of a family receiving news of the death of their son in the war; a monologue called "Vigil Strange I Kept on the Field One Night," about a wake for a dead soldier. The latter poem is tightly constructed and effectively narrated. "A Sight in Camp in the Daybreak Grey and Dim" is almost as metrical and symmetrically divided as a sonnet, though the number of accented syllables in a line varies from four to seven. "The Wound Dresser" is notable both for its autobiographical record of Whitman's changing attitudes toward war during its course and for its "expressive" rhythm, the variations of tempo corresponding to the poet's changing emotions. One poem, "Dirge for Two Veterans," is even stanzaic in form, with a fairly regular metrical system:

> I hear the great drums pounding,
> And the small drums steady whirring,
> And every blow of the great convulsive drums,
> Strikes me through and through.

This might have been written by Whittier or Lowell, but it was the sincere voice of Walt Whitman in "Drum-Taps." If the shrill notes of the fife and the beat of war drums are in marked contrast to his earlier rhythms and verbal music, he did hear them and feel their vibrant message during the war years.

The assassination of President Lincoln almost exactly at the end of the war affected Whitman more deeply than any event in the war itself, but he was not immediately able to write the elegy he felt was needed. He did hastily write a short poem called "Hush'd Be the Camps To-Day" as a gesture of tribute for the funeral, but it was no more than a gesture. Later he wrote "O Captain! My Captain!" in a singsong rhythm in stanza form, even with rhyme and repetend. For triteness of imagery and allegory and monotonous meter, this poem is fortunately unique in *Leaves of Grass*.

The great elegy had to grow slowly in the poet's mind and emotions during the summer of 1865. In the autumn he published a "Sequel" to *Drum-Taps*, which contained "When Lilacs Last in the Dooryard Bloom'd," later included in *Leaves*

of Grass under "Memories of President Lincoln." In some ways
this poem, too, is much nearer the poetic conventions of Victorian literature than are Whitman's earlier poems, but it is also
one of his finest achievements in expressive form. It lacks the
sharp, pungent, startling imagery of "Song of Myself," but it
excels in its verbal music.

In basic concept and major symbols "Lilacs" is in the great
elegy tradition from Greek to modern poets. Richard F. Adams
has declared that by his count,

> out of seventeen devices commonly used in pastoral elegies from
> Bion to Arnold, seven appear in "Lilacs." They are the
> announcement that the speaker's friend or alter ego is dead and
> is to be mourned; the sympathetic mourning of nature, with the
> use of the so-called pathetic fallacy; the placing of flowers on the
> bier; a notice of the irony of nature's revival of life in the spring,
> when the dead man must remain dead; the funeral procession
> with other mourners; the eulogy of the dead man; and the reso-
> lution of the poem in some formula of comfort or reconcili-
> ation.[29]

Although the pastoral setting in combination with such symbols as a star or bird or flower and the use of the springtime to
suggest rebirth are almost the stock-in-trade of elegy poets,
Whitman manages to localize all these devices so successfully
that they seem perfectly natural, unaffected, and appropriate.
Lincoln's death did happen to come in spring—even better (for
symbolism), between Good Friday and Easter. And the funeral
procession in Whitman's elegy is no ordinary procession but
the historic journey of a funeral train which slowly crossed half
a continent as the body of the fallen wartime President was carried to its final resting-place in Springfield, Illinois—actually
passing "Over the breast of spring" in a land of mourning
people.

As it also happened, the evening star was Venus in the spring of 1865, and lilacs were in bloom in Washington, D.C., at the time of the funeral service there, and in Illinois by the time of the final interment. These symbols the poet had given to him by the time and place of the event itself. But the choice of the bird was arbitrary, though quite predictable for the poet who had used the mockingbird so successfully in "Out of the Cradle Endlessly Rocking." But he needed a very special bird for this elegy, one with a supremely sweet song, but not so versatile as the mockingbird. A brown thrasher or a wood thrush might have served, but the hermit thrush was perfect for the role: it has a sweet, poignant song—though heard only in spring, during the breeding season—and it likes seclusion, seldom being seen or heard near human habitations.

The lilac, the star, and spring made a perfect "Trinity" (the fourth symbol; the hermit thrush comes later in the poem), all perennial, and suggestive of rebirth. Some means of defeating death is found in all elegies—as in human psychology, to console the living—but Whitman, and most of the nation, *had* to feel that Lincoln's accomplishments as war President would endure. Any other thought at the end of the long, agonizing war was unbearable; so the President from Illinois was "the western fallen star," but he would "rise again" like Venus, now the evening star, later to become the morning star. The lilac had personal associations for Whitman, for it reminded him of his childhood on Long Island and the bush growing beside his grandparents' farmhouse. And the heart-shaped leaves suggested *love*, a trite symbol in itself, but it could be strengthened by referring to its unforgettable sweet and pleasing perfume. Of the spiked bloom he made no conscious use, though it could have had subconscious phallic associations for him; as Maud Bodkin has observed,[30] the "sprig" of lilac in the poem is similar to the "Golden Bough" in myth (*cf.* Frazer). [31]

Many critics have noticed that "Lilacs" has a musical structure. Once again, Whitman borrows the devices of the recitative and the aria from opera, but the music of this poem is more subtle than the operatic music of "Out of the Cradle." Beginning with the talking voice recalling the time of the lilac in bloom, the star drooping "in the western sky," and "ever-returning spring," the poet thinks of the person whom he will love as long as the seasons last. Though spoken (or possibly chanted), the sentiment, the archetypal images, and the stately rhythm are like a Bach prelude on a great pipe organ. Then the aria gives expression to the seemingly unbearable grief—succeeded by a calming reminiscence of the lilac blooming in the dooryard of an old farmhouse. The broken sprig serves as a memorial and a reminder that love also endures. Then in section 4 the aria of the hermit thrush is heard, singing "Death's outlet song of life"— the voice of nature singing the pathos of death, but also by its song asserting the reality of life.

In section 5 the combined imagery, rhythm, and syntax begin to create empathy of movement and space: the coffin on its journey through the spring landscape, "passing the endless grass," "the yellow-spear'd wheat" risen like Frazer's buried god from its shroud in the earth, passing the apple orchards with their pink and white blossoms.

Night and day journeys a coffin.

The train moves on steadily, pausing now and then at the depots where crowds of mourners have gathered to honor the procession. The metrical beat of "Coffin that passes through lanes and streets," followed by the longer lines of parallelism, creates space-empathy and the finality of its passing as the poet presents his sprig of lilac:

> Here, coffin that passes slowly,
> I give you my sprig of lilac.

In the musical structure the traveling-passing motif alternates, section by section, with the other motifs of lament or star symbolism. As in a symphony, themes, symbols, rhythms are repeated with variations and at the end summarized in a coda.

Section 14 begins the interpretation, the meaning of this death. The poet (or "I") walks with "the knowledge of death" (understanding its meaning) on one side of him and "the thought" (grief for the one who has died) on the other side. Consolation must come from a reconciliation of "knowledge" and "thought," emotion softened by intellectual perception. The bird does not provide this emotional synthesis directly, but in listening to the song of the thrush the poet envisions the "dark mother" ("the old crone rocking the cradle" in the "Cradle" poem) and the song of the thrush takes on the imagery and flowing rhythms of the ocean. Once more it is the ocean—a geographical feature remote from Illinois but deeply imbedded in Whitman's psyche—symbol of death-maternity-birth, which makes death "lovely and soothing."

By section 15 the poet is completely reconciled. But now in a vision he relives the war, with its suffering and death, and feels consoled that it is the living who suffer and not those who fell in battle. If the elegy ended here, it would be as insufferably didactic as one of Longfellow's moralizing poems, but Whitman masterfully returns to the imagery and rhythms of the traveling motif—space and movement empathy—and arrives at a stasis of aesthetic feeling at the end of the long journey. Now at the graveside he can offer "this [his elegy] for his dear sake."

> Lilac and star and bird twined with the chant of my soul,
> There in the fragrant pines and cedars dusk and dim.

Here the syntax (the final inversion of noun and adjectives) brings the last accent on exactly the right syllable with a finality for all eternity.

9

"Passage to India" is the capstone of Whitman's poetic mythology—not his finest poem (he never really surpassed "Song of Myself"), but the one in which all his theories of the function of poetry and his own ambition to be a "poet-prophet" received final and most nearly coherent expression. One might even say that here he comes nearest to being the "epic" poet some critics[32] have tried to find in his *Leaves of Grass,* but he is a democratized Milton rather than an American Homer.

The seventeenth-century Puritan wrote his Christian epic "to justify the ways of God to man," by which he meant to exonerate God from *injustice* in expelling Adam and Eve from the Garden of Eden, and to reconcile mankind to its inherited curse of "original sin." Whitman's purpose is not so specifically theological—though it is theological, too, in a broader, more prophetic sense than Milton's, for he also believes that God created the earth (the "vast Rondure, swimming in space") for a specific purpose, and that His will has secretly propelled the human race through its tumultous history. By understanding and accepting this plan, mankind can now, Whitman intimates, co-operate in its culminating glory. The poet, the "true son of God," is the one who can comprehend the plan and "justify" it to mankind—Whitman uses the word three times, as if to emphasize his Miltonic program.

This is, indeed, a vast program, but Whitman had announced in his 1855 Preface: "The poets of the kosmos advance through all interpositions and coverings and turmoils and stratagems to first principles." More concisely: the "poet of the kosmos" should *indicate the path between reality and the soul*.[33] Emerson taught that man had somehow become separated from nature,[34] and that salvation lay in healing the breach, which he, like Whitman, strove to accomplish. Whitman's Adam, as we observed of his "Children of Adam" poems,[35] was prelapsarian; yet Whitman believed no less firmly than Emerson in the need for restoring a lost harmony between man and nature, the latter animated by the breath of Deity.

However, in spite of Whitman's ambition to compete with Milton, his "Passage to India" can hardly be called an epic poem except for its range of subject, and he himself intended it only for an introduction to a collection which would have (if ever completed) something like the body of an epic. In a preface to *As a Strong Bird on Pinions Free* (1872), Whitman revealed his intention to let *Leaves of Grass* stand (in the 1871 edition) as a completed book, "an epic of Democracy,"[36] and to start a new volume of poems with a more pronounced "religious purpose." In the same year he published a small volume entitled *Passage to India*, which he added to *Leaves of Grass* in 1876, and retained thereafter as a thin cluster. In his 1876 preface he explained that "*Passage to India*, and its cluster, are but freer vent and fuller expression to what, from the first, and so on throughout, more or less lurks in all my writings, underneath every page, every line, every where."[37] This poem, then, might be said to epitomize *Leaves of Grass*, not only the body of poems published by 1871, but also those that Whitman planned in future years to add to it for "fuller expression" of its basic intent.

"Passage to India" begins as a topical poem, celebrating three recent epoch-making events: the opening of the Suez Canal, the spanning of the North American continent by railroad, and the completion of the Atlantic cable.[38] Whitman was not alone in looking upon these great engineering feats—"Our modern wonders, (the antique ponderous Seven outvied,)"—as at long last making possible an age of universal peace and brotherhood among the peoples of the world. He begins his poem by "Singing of the great achievements of the present," but they remind him that "the present [is] after all but a growth out of the past"; and in section 2 he turns to the past, takes passage in fantasy to India, the cradle of mankind (as historians then assumed), origin of the oldest myths and fables, of "deep diving bibles" and "the elder religions":

> O you temples fairer than lilies pour'd over by the rising sun!
> O you fables spurning the known, eluding the hold of the
>   known, mounting to heaven!
> You lofty and dazzling towers, pinnacl'd, red as roses,
>   burnish'd with gold!
> Towers of fables immortal fashion'd from mortal dreams!
> You too I welcome and fully the same as the rest!
> You too with joy I sing.

Looking back, he sees "God's purpose from the first":

> The earth to be spann'd, connected by network,
>   races, neighbors, to marry and be given in marriage,
> The oceans to be cross'd, the distance brought near,
> The lands to be welded together.

Therefore, "A worship new I sing," joining to his celebration of explorers, architects, and machinists, the worship of "God's purpose" revealed in their achievements. Once more using musical structure, Whitman envisions the material accomplishments in images of the contemporary newspaper accounts. In section 3 he sees and hears "the locomotives rushing and roaring, and the shrill steamwhistle" reverberating on the plains, over the rivers, through the mountains clear across the continent to the Pacific Ocean. In section 4 he salutes the explorers who in seeking a passage to India discovered America and hastened the end of "man's long probation." Section 5, a paean to the "vast Rondure swimming in space, / Cover'd all over with visible power and beauty," was actually written before the other sections of "Passage to India," and it contains the central idea of the whole poem. In his fantasy of looking down upon the earth from a point high in space (anticipating the astronauts of the twentieth century), he feels that he begins to comprehend the Divine "inscrutable purpose, some hidden prophetic intention . . .":

Down from the garden of Asia descending radiating,
Adam and Eve appear, then their myriad progeny after them,
Wandering, yearning, curious, with restless explorations,
With questionings, baffled, formless, feverish, with never
    happy hearts.
With that sad incessant refrain, *Wherefore unsatisfied soul?* and
    Whither O mocking life?

Ah who shall soothe these feverish children?
Who justify these restless explorations?
Who speak the secret of impassive earth?
Who bind it to us? what is this separate Nature so unnatural?
What is this earth to our affections? (unloving earth,
    without a throb to answer ours,
Cold earth, the place of graves.)

Yet soul be sure the first intent remains, and shall be carried
    out,
Perhaps even now the time has arrived.

Whitman had always striven to be the Orphic poet, but he had never before had a subject which enabled him to make so clear an application of this role, and the application is one which educators and philosophers of the twentieth century were to seek desperately: how to humanize the discoveries and inventions of the explorers, scientists, and engineers. Whitman believes this to be the function of the poet, whom he calls the "true son of God" not because he is in competition with the Christian Son of God but because, like Christ, his life is to be devoted to explaining God's plan of redemption for the human race:

> Then not your deeds only O voyagers, O scientists and
>   inventors, shall be justified,
> All these hearts as of fretted children shall be sooth'd,
> All affection shall be responded to, the secret shall be told,
> All these separations and gaps shall be taken up and hook'd
>   and link'd together,
> The whole earth, this cold, impassive, voiceless earth, shall
>   be completely justified,
> Trinitas divine shall be gloriously accomplish'd and
>   compacted by the true son of God, the poet,
> (He shall indeed pass the straits and conquer the mountains,
> He shall double the cape of Good Hope to some purpose,)
> Nature and Man shall be disjoin'd and diffused no more,
> The true son of God shall absolutely fuse them.

Christ preached his Gospel, performed miracles with His Father's help, and tried to prepare men and women for God's Kingdom. This modern poet-son of God has a similar mission to persuade his readers to *see* and comprehend the Utopia in which "All affection shall be responded to," and the breach between man and nature shall be completely healed, "hook'd and link'd together." The poet (artist) works by creating empathy: his readers must see and feel so intensely that they will accept the poet's vision and act upon it. Accordingly, section 6 is a vision of ancient times and people, a montage of human history. In this vision, "the Admiral," Christopher Columbus, appears on the stage at the right time and performs his epical deeds. Though in his personal life he was rewarded by "slander, poverty, and death," he is like the seed planted in the ground (or Frazer's buried god).[39]

> Lies the seed unreck'd for centuries in the ground?
> lo, to God's due occasion,
> Uprising in the night, it sprouts, blooms,
> And fills the earth with use and beauty.

Of course, one reason for Whitman's strong identification with Columbus was his feeling that he, also a discoverer in the realm of literature and likewise slandered and neglected, would some day be recognized like Columbus and that his *Leaves of Grass* would sprout and bloom and fill "the earth with use and beauty."

Beginning in section 2, Whitman invokes his "soul" to take passage with him back to India and the beginning of history, though until section 7 the invocations are little more than a literary device. But in section 7 this backward journey becomes more personal and psychologically motivated. The poet is still in fantasy circumnavigating the world, back to "primal thought," the "realms of budding bibles," back to "innocent [prelapsarian] intuitions," but this journey becomes in section 8 a quest for more than an imaginative understanding of man's intellectual and religious origins. The poet's spiritual self begins more and more to resemble the Christian concept of "soul." Whitman is now thinking more of his own approaching physical death than of the return to the India of "budding bibles," and his poem becomes a religious lyric—meditative, prayerful, a searching for personal consolation.

> O we can wait no longer,
> We too take ship O soul,
> Joyous we too launch out on trackless seas,
> Fearless for unknown shores on waves of ecstasy to sail,
> Amid the wafting winds, (thou pressing me to thee, I thee to me, O soul,)
> Caroling free, singing our song of God,
> Chanting our chant of pleasant exploration.

> With laugh and many a kiss,
> (Let others deprecate, let others weep for sin, remorse, humiliation,)
> O soul thou pleasest me, I thee.

> Ah more than any priest O soul we too believe in God,
> But with the mystery of God we dare not dally.

> O soul thou pleasest me, I thee,
> Sailing these seas or on the hills, or waking in the night,
> Thoughts, silent thoughts, of Time and Space and Death, like waters flowing.
> Bear me indeed as through the regions infinite,
> Whose air I breathe, whose ripples hear, lave me all over,
> Bathe me O god in thee, mounting to thee,
> I and my soul to range in range of thee.

The God to whom the poet prays is of course the same creator of the "vast Rondure" of section 5:

> O Thou transcendent,
> Nameless, the fibre and the breath,

Light of the light, shedding forth universes, thou centre of them,
Thou mightier centre of the true, the good, the loving,
Thou moral, spiritual fountain—affection's source—thou reservoir,
(O pensive soul of me—O thirst unsatisfied—waitest not there?
Waitest not haply for us somewhere there the Comrade per-
    fect?)
Thou pulse—thou motive of stars, suns, systems,
That, circling, move in order, safe, harmonious,
Athwart the shapeless vastnesses of space,
How should I think, how breathe a single breath, how speak,
    if, out of myself,
I could not launch, to those, superior universes?

This "spiritual fountain" concept of God has traces of
Buddhism (God is an unknowable mystery), of Deism (God
the maker and mover), of Pantheism (God as breath and
pulse), but it is no less anthropomorphic: God is "the Comrade perfect" (a "Calamus" motif) and the "Elder Brother,"
into whose arms the Younger Brother (the poet) melts, almost
as in a Christian heaven. However, this final journey with the
soul also resembles the Vedantic return to Brahman, because
the poet's soul, his "actual Me," masters the orbs (stars and
planets), mates with Time, smiles at Death, and fills "the vast-
ness of Space"—see Chari's thesis (page 141).

In section 9 the poet asks rhetorically whether his soul is prepared for such flights to "more than India," to sound "below
the Sanskrit and the Vedas." That is, to plunge to the ultimate
origin of the intuitions of these sacred writings. Convinced that
it is, the poet then bids it to unleash its "bent" (power held in
reserve for this purpose), to cut the hawsers, unfurl the sails,
and steer for "deep waters only"—into "the seas of God."

The imagery and rhythms of *flowing* are always prominent in
Whitman's poetry when he treats the subject of death (as in

"The Sleepers," "Out of the Cradle Endlessly Rocking," the latter part of "When Lilacs Last . . ."), and the flowing motif is very effective in some lines (". . . lave me all over, / Bathe me O God . . ."), but at times they become almost a psychological reflex. Section 9 is extremely rhetorical, impassioned, and urgent, but the sailing motif barely escapes (if it does) the triteness of Whitman's ship-of-state cliché in "O Captain! My Captain!" And the poet's identification with Columbus echoes the words of Washington Irving's biography of Columbus (a passage once recited by thousands of school children), "O farther, farther, farther sail!"

"Passage to India" is virtually two poems, the Miltonic "justificaton" of God's cosmic plan in the first six sections, and in the last three the poet's weariness with the life of "eating and drinking" and his intense longing to become all-spirit. He is still conscious of himself as two,[40] his soul and himself, "thou and me," but the "me" is no longer capable of the physical ecstasy so marvelously expressed in "Song of Myself" and the earlier poems.

"Prayer of Columbus," which Whitman placed immediately after "Passage to India" in Leaves of Grass, is almost a continuation of "Passage to India." The poet identifies so strongly with the "batter'd, wreck'd old man" that Columbus's prayer is his prayer.

> My hands, my limbs grow nerveless,
> My brain feels rack'd, bewilder'd,
> Let the old timbers part, I will not part,
> I will cling fast to Thee, O God, though the waves buffet me,
> Thee, Thee at least I know.

This prayer, however, concerns Whitman's Leaves of Grass as well as his biography. As Blodgett and Bradley comment in a

footnote to "Prayer of Columbus" in their Reader's Edition of
Leaves of Grass: ". . . the deep purport linking this poem with
'Passage to India' is the poet's profoundly felt need of divine
sanction for his work, his body of poetry which had come from
the 'potent, felt, interior command,' for which he, as Columbus, prays."[41]

The group titles following "Passage to India" indicate this
same "felt need": "Whispers of Heavenly Death," "From
Noon to Starry Night," "Songs of Parting," and the two
Annexes: "Sands at Seventy" and "Good-Bye My Fancy." No
poet was ever more aware of his mortality. And yet the dignity
and courage which he exhibited after his paralysis save these
old-age poems from sentimentality or morbidity. Many of the
"Whispers of Heavenly Death" he had heard (and written)
long before this period, and the same is true of his "Parting"
and "Noon to Starry Night" poems. In fact, he had been preparing to depart ever since 1860 (*cf.* "So Long!"). But the
poems of the Annexes were actually written by a septuage-
narian. Most of these are brief, such as a two-line epigram, a
short aphorism, or a single image expanded into a symbol, as in
"A Font of Type," "My Canary Bird," waves, tides, dusk, etc.
To the last he lived in memory and "fancy" near the sounds
and sights and smells of the ocean, which, as we have many
times seen, had symbolical values for him.

Roger Asselineau makes an acute observation on the major
difference between Whitman's poems in the earlier editions of
Leaves of Grass and his old-age poems. In the early poems,

> Then, "great thoughts of space and eternity fill" him and he
> thinks of all the globes of the past and the future, of the immen-
> sity of the universe. Yet, as he grew older, the dimensions both
> of his subjects and of his poems shrank. He needed no less than

the whole earth at the beginning of his career; in his old age, he was satisfied with a flower, a bird, a street, a printer's case—and a few lines. And yet, these humble vignettes still imply and suggest the rest of the world in the manner of the Japanese hokkus of the best period. "The first dandelion" reminds us of the everlastingness of life, the canary in its cage celebrates the "joi de vivre" in its own way; all mankind walks up and down Broadway and the "font of type" contains in its latent form all the passions of men. His imagination has lost its former vigor, but his glance has remained as piercing as ever and his sight still carries to the utmost confines of the universe:

> Distances balk'd . . .
> I feel the sky, the prairies vast—I feel
>   the mighty northern lakes,
> I feel the ocean and the forest—somehow I feel
>   the globe itself swift-swimming in space . . .

he exclaimed as late as 1890.[42]

One way in which Whitman did not change with age was his continuing to think of himself as two, me and "the real me" in "Song of Myself," his soul and himself in "Passage to India," himself and his "Fancy" in the final poem of his book, "Good-Bye My Fancy." And he was also equally concerned to the end about another duality, himself (or himself in his book) and his reader. Sometime in 1891 he wrote "For Us Two, Reader Dear":

> Simple, spontaneous, curious, two souls interchanging,
> With the original testimony for us continued to the last.

This imaginary reader was the "Comrade perfect" for whom he had sought and sung throughout *Leaves of Grass*.

Notes

1. There is a legend that the first *Leaves of Grass* went on sale July 4, 1855, but the first newspaper advertisement appeared in the New York *Tribune* on July 6. See G. W. Allen, *The Solitary Singer: A Critical Biography of Walt Whitman* (New York, 1955), 149.

2. Quoted in supplement to the second issue of the 1855 *Leaves of Grass*; reprinted in *Leaves of Grass Imprints* (Boston, 1860), 36–38.

3. *Imprints*, 36–37.

4. *Ibid.*, 37. The first sentence reads "without," but the context implies "with comical success."

5. *A Leaf of Grass from Shady Hill, With a Review of Walt Whitman's Leaves of Grass Written by Charles Eliot Norton in 1855* (Cambridge, Mass., 1928).

6. Edmund Wilson, ed., *The Shock of Recognition* (New York, 1943).

7. *Imprints*, 3.

8. *Ibid.*, 5.

9. *Ibid.*, 6

10. *Ibid.*, 35.

11. *Ibid.*, 20–27.

12. *Ibid.*, 24.

13. The controversy began with a letter of inquiry from John Addington Symonds in 1890. See *Solitary Singer*, 535; also G. W. Allen, *Walt Whitman as Man, Poet, and Legend* (Carbondale, Ill., 1961), 109 ff.

14. In conversation with the author of this book, but implied in the Introduction to *Walt Whitman's Leaves of Grass: The First (1855) Edition*, ed. Malcolm Cowley (New York, 1959), xxxvii.

15. Acknowledged in *In Re Walt Whitman*, ed. Literary Executors (Philadelphia, 1893), 13, 17.

16. *Imprints*, 38–41; *In Re*, 27–32.

17. Hero of B. A. Baker's drama, *A Glance at New York in 1848; Solitary Singer*, 63.

18. Barrett Wendell, *A Literary History of America* (New York, 1901), 465.

19. *Ibid.*, 468 ff.

20. *Ibid.*, 479.

CHAPTER II

1. Whitman's confession of Emerson's influence, see J. T. Trowbridge, *My Own Story* (Boston, 1903), 360. Studies: J. B. Moore, "The Master of Whitman," *Studies in Philology*, XXIII, 77–89 (January 1926); Clarence Gohdes, "Whitman and Emerson," *Sewanee Review*, XXXVII, 79–93 (January 1929); Leon Howard, "For a Critique of Whitman's Transcendentalism," *Modern Language Notes*, XLVII, 79–85 (February 1932).

2. Nearly every biographer marvels at the almost unbelievable contrast between Whitman's poems of the 1840s and those in the first edition of *Leaves of Grass* and tries to find explanations.

3. William James, *Varieties of Religious Experience* (New York and London, 1902), 379–429. (Reprint 1963 by University Books, same pagination.)

4. *Ibid.*, 396–399.

5. G. W. Allen, *The Solitary Singer* (New York, 1955), 7–8, 11–12.

6. Walt Whitman, *Prose Works 1892*, ed. Floyd Stovall, in *Collected Writings of Walt Whitman* (New York University Press, 1964), I, 7.

7. See *Solitary Singer*, 22.

8. *Ibid.*, 30.

9. For a contemporary account, see Theodore Parker's *Life and Correspondence*, ed. John Weiss (New York, 1964), II, 125 ff.

10. *The Ruins; or Meditation on the Revolutions of Empires*, by C. F. Volney (New York, Calvin Blanchard, n.d.—first published in 1793, rev. 1797), 23.

11. *A Few Days in Athens, Being the Translation of a Greek Manuscript Discovered in Heraculaneum* [fiction], by Frances Wright (New York, Peter Eckler, n.d.—dedicated to Jeremy Bentham in 1822). For Whitman's use of this book, see David Goodale, "Some of Walt Whitman's Borrowings," *American Literature*, X, 202–213 (May 1938).

12. Whitman's holograph outline is in the Library of Congress, Manuscript Division; discussed in *Solitary Singer*, 139–140.

13. *A Few Days*, 135.

14. G. W. Allen, "Biblical Echoes in Whitman's Works," *American Literature*, VI, 302–315 (November 1934).

15. "Shirval, A Tale of Jerusalem," in *The Half-Breed and Other Stories of Walt Whitman, Now First Collected*, by Thomas Ollive Mabbott (New York, 1927), 79–85.

16. Preface to 1855 edition reprinted in *Leaves of Grass: Comprehensive Reader's Edition*, ed. Harold W. Blodgett and Sculley Bradley (New York University Press, 1965), 714.

17. *Democratic Vistas*, reprinted in *Prose Works 1892* (ed. Stovall), II, 406.

18. Whitman's newspaper editorials showed considerable interest in Dickens, and in 1842 he defended the author of Boz. *Walt Whitman of the New York Aurora: Editor at Twenty-Two*, ed. Joseph Jay Rubin and Charles H. Brown (State College, Pa., 1950), 114–116.

19. Cf. *Prose Works 1892* (ed. Stovall), I, 521–523; II, 712.

20. Esther Shephard developed this thesis in *Walt Whitman's Pose* (New York, 1938).

21. Haniel Long, *Walt Whitman and the Springs of Courage* (Santa Fe, N.M., 1938).

22. *Prose Works 1892* (ed. Stovall), Shakespeare poisonous to democracy, II, 388; feudalistic, 475, 490; early love of, 722, 725, 756; essay: "Shakespeare for America," 674–675.

23. Quoted from Whitman's extract, but also reprinted by T. P. Whipple from *Boston Miscellany*, February 1843, in *Essays and Reviews* (New York, 1848), I, 73–77.

24. *The Correspondence of Henry David Thoreau*, ed. Walter Harding and Carl Bode (New York, 1958), 445.

25. "A Backward Glance O'er Travel'd Roads," Preface to *November Boughs*, 1888; *Prose Works 1892* (ed. Stovall), II, 721–722.

26. Lord Strangford, "Walt Whitman," *The Pall Mall Gazette*, February 16, 1866; reprinted in *A Selection from the Writings of Viscount Strangford* (London, 1869), II, 297 ff.; see also Harold Blodgett, *Walt Whitman in England* (Ithaca, N.Y., 1934), 198.

27. Gabriel Sarrazin, "Walt Whitman," in *La Renaissance de la Poésie Anglaise, 1798–1889* (Paris, 1889); translation in *In Re Walt Whitman*, ed. Literary Executors of Walt Whitman (Philadelphia, 1893), 159–194.

28. Edward Carpenter, *Days with Walt Whitman* (London, 1906), 94–102.

29. *Ibid.*, 250.

30. William A. Guthrie, *Walt Whitman the Camden Sage* (Cincinnati, 1897), 25.

31. Summarized, G. W. Allen, *Walt Whitman Handbook* (Chicago, 1946), 459–462.

32. V. K. Chari, *Whitman in the Light of Vedantic Mysticism* (Lincoln, Neb., 1964), 18.

33. T. R. Rajasekharaiah, *Walt Whitman's Roots and Leaves* (Rutherford, N.J., 1970), believes he has found internal evidence of extensive borrowing and adaptation (even unacknowledged appropriation) of ideas, phrases, and passages from Indian literature which Whitman read in translation or in English interpretations.

34. John Stafford, *The Literary Criticism of "Young America," A Study in the Relationship of Politics and Literature, 1837–1850* (Berkeley, Calif., 1952). See *Solitary Singer,* 127–130.

35. *Ibid.,* 67.

36. *Ibid.,* 118.

37. Many of Whitman's editorials in the *Eagle* were collected by Cleveland Rodgers and John Black in *The Gathering of the Forces* (New York, 1920), 2 vols. A study of Whitman's editorials: Thomas Brasher, *Walt Whitman, Editor of the Brooklyn Eagle* (Detroit, 1970).

38. *In Re,* 13.

39. *Leaves of Grass: Comprehensive Reader's Edition,* 710.

40. See testimony of George Whitman, *In Re,* 35.

41. *Uncollected Poetry and Prose of Walt Whitman,* ed. Emory Holloway (New York, 1921), II, 63.

42. *Ibid.,* II, 90.

43. *Ibid.,* II, 65.

44. *Ibid.,* II, 66.

45. *Ibid.*

46. *Ibid.*

47. *Ibid.,* II, 67.

48. *Ibid.*

49. *Ibid.,* II, 68.

50. *Ibid.*

51. *Ibid.,* 79–80.

52. *Ibid.,* 81.

53. *In Re,* 16.

54. Edwin H. Miller, *Walt Whitman's Poetry: A Psychological Journey* (Boston and New York, 1969), 37, passim.

55. Jean Catel, *Walt Whitman: La Naissance du poète* (Paris, 1929), 38–39.

56. Remark to Horace Traubel, in one of the volumes of *With Walt Whitman in Camden*—exact page not located.

57. *Leaves of Grass: Comprehensive Reader's Edition,* 751.

58. Edward Hungerford, "Walt Whitman and His Chart of Bumps," *American Literature,* II, 350–384 (January 1931).

59. Edwin H. Miller, 71–72.

CHAPTER III

1. See Chapter I, note 2.

2. Oscar Triggs, "The Growth of 'Leaves of Grass,'" *The Complete Writings of Walt Whitman* (New York and London, 1902), X, 102.

3. R. M. Bucke, *Walt Whitman* (Philadelphia, 1883), 155.

4. Mark Van Doren, "The Poet," in *Walt Whitman: Man, Poet, Philosopher*. Three Lectures Presented Under the Auspices of the Gertrude Clarke Whittall Poetry and Literature Fund (Library of Congress, 1955), 19.

5. *Leaves of Grass: Comprehensive Reader's Edition*, ed. Harold W. Blodgett and Sculley Bradley (New York University Press, 1965), 575.

6. Notably Malcolm Cowley—see Chapter I, note 14.

7. Frederik Schyberg, *Walt Whitman* (Copenhagen, 1933) was one of the first; later, Roy Harvey Pearce, Introduction to *Leaves of Grass*: Facsimile Edition of the 1860 Text (Ithaca, N.Y., 1961).

8. Part of *The Collected Writings of Walt Whitman* (New York University Press)—announced for 1970.

9. See Chapter I, note 14; Doubleday, 1954, text without editorial apparatus.

10. The Eakins Press, New York, 1966.

11. Horace Traubel, *With Walt Whitman in Camden* (New York, 1908), II, 471.

12. See Ralph Adimari, "Leaves of Grass—First Edition," *American Book Collector*, V, 150–152 (May–June 1934).

13. *Ibid.*, 149, 177.

14. Willie T. Weathers, "Whitman's Poetic Translations of His 1855 Preface," *American Literature*, XIX, 21–40 (March 1947).

15. Introduction to 1855 *Leaves of Grass*, x (see Chapter I, note 14).

16. *Ibid.*, xxxvi.

17. *The Solitary Singer*, 151.

18. Emerson's letter has often been quoted, though usually slightly inaccurately from a transcription Whitman made; see photograph of the letter in G. W. Allen, *Walt Whitman* (Wayne State University Press, 1969), [63].

19. *Leaves of Grass* (Brooklyn, 1856), 346.

20. *Ibid.*, 351–352.

21. Ed. Edward F. Grier, *The Eighteenth Presidency!* (University of Kansas Press, 1956). Copies exist only in proof sheets (one set in Library of Congress).

22. *Ibid.*, 22.

23. *Ibid.*, 30.

24. *Ibid.*, 44.

25. *Leaves of Grass* (Brooklyn, 1856), 352.

26. See Chapter II, note 34.

27. *Leaves of Grass* (Brooklyn, 1856), 355–356.

28. See Chapter II, note 14.

29. Relations with Fowler and Wells, *Solitary Singer*, 176, 178, 207, 217.

30. Text of first version: *A Child's Reminiscence by Walt Whitman*, collected by Thomas O. Mabbott and Rollo G. Silver, with an Introduction and Notes (Seattle, 1930).

31. *The Solitary Singer*, 236–237.

32. Frederik Schyberg, *Walt Whitman*, translated by Evie Allison Allen (New York, 1950), 151 (original, Copenhagen, 1933).

33. See note 32, above.

34. Pearce, xx (see note 7, above).

35. D. H. Lawrence, *Studies in Classic American Literature* (New York, 1951 [first edition, 1923]), 177.

36. Fredson Bowers, "Whitman's Manuscripts for the Original 'Calamus' Poems," *Studies in Bibliography* (University of Virginia), VI, 257–265 (1953–54).

37. Title changed to "Elemental Drifts" in the 1867 *Leaves of Grass*; present title in the 1881 edition.

38. These lines were restored in 1867.

39. Fredson Bowers, ed., *Whitman's Manuscripts: Leaves of Grass (1860): A Parallel Text* (Chicago, 1955), xxxv.

40. See *Solitary Singer*, 267, 569 note 25.

41. *Ibid.*, 265–266.

42. *Ibid.*

43. Fullest study: George L. Sixbey, "Chanting the Square Deific—A Study in Whitman's Religion," *American Literature*, IX, 171–195 (May 1937).

44. Whitman's ideas for this poem had been crystallizing for ten years—see Sixbey (above).

45. Whitman changed the Italian *Spirito Santo* (masculine gender), "Holy Spirit," from Latin *Spiritus Sanctus*, to the feminine form. Some critics have thought Whitman's spelling an ignorant error, but his *Santa Spirita* is not so much the Christian "Holy Spirit" as *Life* (note stanza 4), for which the feminine form seems more appropriate.

46. See *The Solitary Singer*, 274.

47. *Walt Whitman's Workshop: A Collection of Unpublished Manuscripts*, ed. Clifton Joseph Furness (Cambridge, Mass., 1928), 137.

48. *Ibid.*, 127–130.

49. *Walt Whitman's Blue Book: the 1860–61 Leaves of Grass Containing His Manuscript Additions and Revisions*, ed. Arthur Golden (New York Public Library, 1968).

50. *Ibid.*, II, lviii–lv; *Solitary Singer*, 344–350.

51. Opinion held by Golden (see note 49, above) and Allen in *The Solitary Singer*.
52. *Walt Whitman's Blue Book*, I, 27.
53. *The Solitary Singer*, 3[ ].
54. A. C. Swinburne, *William Blake* (London, 1868), 337.
55. See N. F. Adkins, "Emerson and the Bardic Tradition," *PMLA*, LXIII, 662–677 (June 1 48).
56. *Prose Works 18[ ]*, ed. Floyd Stovall (New York University Press, 1964), II, 365.
57. *Ibid.*, II, 366.
58. *Ibid.*, 369–37[ ]
59. *Ibid.*, 379 ff.
60. Reprinted by Harold W. Blodgett and Sculley Bradley, eds., in *Leaves of Grass: Comprehensive Reader's Edition* (New York, 1965), 739.
61. *Ibid.*, 743.
62. To Ellen O'Connor; *The Solitary Singer*, 458.
63. *Studies in Classic American Literature*, 184.
64. W. S. Kennedy, *The Fight of a Book for the World* (London, 1926), 181.
65. *The Solitary Singer*, 496.
66. *Ibid.*, 499.
67. *Prose Works 1892* (ed. Stovall), I, 26 *passim*.
68. *Ibid.*, 92.
69. *Ibid.*, I, 5–12.
70. Reprinted, *Ibid.*, II, 711–732.
71. Accurate details of the "deathbed" edition will be given by Sculley Bradley and Harold W. Blodgett in their *Variorum Leaves of Grass*.
72. See note 71, above.

CHAPTER IV

1. Ferner Nuhn, "Leaves of Grass Viewed as an Epic," *Arizona Quarterly*, VII, 324–338 (Winter 1951); James E. Miller, "America's Epic," in *A Critical Guide to Leaves of Grass* (Chicago, 1957), 256–261; Roy Harvey Pearce, *The Continuity of American Poetry* (Princeton, 1961), 69–83.
2. Gay Wilson Allen and Charles T. Davis, eds., *Walt Whitman's Poems* (New York, 1955), 26 ff.
3. So called by R. M. Bucke, *Walt Whitman* (Philadelphia, 1883), 183–185.
4. R. W. Emerson, "Nature" (1836), Section IV, "Language."

5. *Ibid.*

6. "A Backward Glance O'er Travel'd Roads," *Prose Works* 1892 (ed. Stovall), II, 731.

7. *Ibid.*, 712.

8. J. T. Trowbridge, *My Own Story* (Boston, 1903), 360.

9. See Chapter I, note 14.

10. G. W. Allen, "The Two Poets of Leaves of Grass," in *Patterns of Commitment in American Literature*, ed. Marston LaFrance (Toronto, 1967), 53–72.

11. See p. 14.

12. Harold W. Blodgett and Sculley Bradley, eds., *Leaves of Grass: Comprehensive Reader's Edition* (New York University Press, 1965), 751.

13. *Prose Works* 1892 (ed. Stovall), II, 715.

14. See G. W. Allen, *The Solitary Singer: A Critical Biography of Walt Whitman* (New York, 1955), 219.

15. On "space empathy": G. W. Allen, "The Influence of Space on the American Imagination," in *Essays on American Literature in Honor of Jay B. Hubbell* (Duke University Press, 1967), 329–342.

16. *Leaves of Grass: Comprehensive Reader's Edition*, 715.

17. See, *e.g.*, Cowley, *op. cit.*, Allen, *The Solitary Singer*, and Chari, discussed in Chapter V.

18. William James, *Varieties of Religious Experience* (London and New York, 1902), 395.

19. *Ibid.*, 396.

20. See pp. 35–36.

21. *With Walt Whitman in Camden: April 8—September 14, 1889*, by Horace Traubel, ed. Gertrude Traubel (Southern Illinois University Press, 1964), 376.

22. Edwin H. Miller, *Walt Whitman's Poetry: A Psychological Journey* (Boston and New York, 1969), 20.

23. *Ibid.*, 23.

24. Section 33, lines 840–43.

25. D. H. Lawrence, *Studies in Classic American Literature* (New York, 1951), 181.

26. *Ibid.*, 177.

27. *Ibid.*

28. Frederik Schyberg, *Walt Whitman*, translated by Evie Allison Allen (New York, 1950), 167.

29. Edwin Miller, see note 22 above.

30. James E. Miller (see note 1, above), 6–35.

31. *Ibid.*, 10.

32. *Ibid.*, 78.
33. Richard Chase, *Walt Whitman Reconsidered* (New York, 1955), 58.
34. *Ibid.*, 60.
35. *Ibid.*
36. *Ibid.*
37. *Ibid.*, 64.
38. *Ibid.*
39. *Ibid.*, 78.
40. *Ibid.*, 82.
41. *Ibid.*, 72.
42. V. K. Chari, *Whitman in the Light of Vedantic Mysticism* (University of Nebraska Press, 1964), 12.
43. *Ibid.*, 55.
44. See I, note 33.
45. Chari, 75.
46. *Ibid.*, 95.
47. *Ibid.*, 107.
48. *Ibid.*, 108.
49. *Ibid.*, 118.
50. *Ibid.*, 139.
51. *Uncollected Poetry and Prose of Walt Whitman*, ed. Emory Holloway (New York, 1921), II, 69–70.
52. "Democratic Vistas," in *Prose Works 1892* (ed. Stovall), II, 417.
53. Chari, 142.
54. *Ibid.*, 143.
55. See Chapter I, note 33.
56. Jeevan Publications, Bangalore, India, 1966.
57. James E. Miller, Jr., Karl Shapiro, and Bernice Slote, *Start with the Sun: Studies in Cosmic Poetry* (University of Nebraska Press, 1960).
58. E. F. Carlisle, "Walt Whitman: The Drama of Identity," *Quarterly for Literature and the Arts*, X, 259–276 (Fall 1968), 261.
59. *Ibid.*
60. *Ibid.*, 262.
61. *Ibid.*, 263.
62. R. W. B. Lewis, *Trials of the Word: Essays in American Literature and the Humanistic Tradition* (Yale University Press, 1965).
63. Carlisle, 262, note 5.
64. *Ibid.*, 264.
65. *Ibid.*
66. *Ibid.*, 266, note 8.

67. *Ibid.*
68. *Ibid.*, 268.
69. *Ibid.*, 269.
70. *Ibid.*, 275.
71. *Ibid.*, 276.

CHAPTER V

1. See p. 5.
2. *Prose Works 1892*, ed. Flod Stovall (New York University Press, 1963), I, 284.
3. *Leaves of Grass: Comprehensive Reader's Edition*, eds. Harold W. Blodgett and Sculley Bradley (New York University Press, 1965), 728.
4. "The Poet" (1844), beginning of eighth paragraph.
5. *Leaves of Grass: Comprehensive Reader's Edition*, 714.
6. Samuel Taylor Coleridge, "Shakespeare, a Poet Generally," in *Essays and Lectures on Shakespeare and Some Other Old Dramatists* (London: Everyman Library, n.d.), 46–47.
7. *Biographia Literaria*, Chap. XIV.
8. Remy de Gourmont, *Le Problème du Style: La nouvelle Poésie Française* (Paris, 1902), 159.
Francis Vielé-Griffin was an American expatriate (born on Long Island) who became one of the French Symbolist poets.
9. See G. W. Allen, *American Prosody* (New York, 1935, 1966), 221 ff.
10. G. W. Allen, "Biblical Echoes in Whitman's Works," *American Literature*, VI, 302–315 (November 1934).
11. Jannaccone, *La Poesia di Walt Whitman e L'Evoluzione delle Forme Ritmiche* (Torino, 1898), 67.
12. *Ibid.*
13. *Ibid.*
14. C. M. Bowra, *Primitive Song* (London, 1962), 60.
15. *Ibid.*, 63.
16. *The Modern Reader's Bible: Presented in Modern Literary Form*, ed. Richard G. Moulton (New York, 1922), 802.
17. "Whitman in Israel," in *Walt Whitman Abroad*, ed. G. W. Allen (Syracuse University Press, 1955), 235–236.
18. See G. W. Allen, *The Solitary Singer* (New York, 1955), 157 ff.
19. Introduction to *Leaves of Grass: The First (1855) Edition*, ed. Malcolm Cowley (New York, 1959), x.
20. R. M. Bucke, *Walt Whitman* (Philadelphia, 1883), 171–172.
21. R. M. Bucke, *Cosmic Consciousness* (New York, 1923—many reprints).

22. Edwin H. Miller, *Walt Whitman's Poetry*: A *Psychological Journey* (Boston and New York, 1969), 73.

23. See Chapter IV, note 21.

24. In *Thus Spake Zarathustra*, the illusion of the weak.

25. Edwin H. Miller, 201–202.

26. A *Child's Reminiscence* by *Walt Whitman*, collected by Thomas O. Mabbott and Rollo G. Silver, with Introduction and Notes (Seattle, 1930), 41.

27. *Ibid.*, 37–40.

28. *The Solitary Singer*, 112–115.

29. R. P. Adams, "Whitman's 'Lilacs' and the Tradition of Pastoral Elegy," *PMLA*, LXXII, 479 (June 1957).

30. Maud Bodkin, *Archetypal Patterns in Poetry* (London, 1934), 130–131.

31. Sir James George Fraser, *The Golden Bough*: A *Study in Magic and Religion* [abridged edition] (New York, 1942), 701 ff.

32. See Chapter IV, note 1.

33. Preface, 1855 edition, *Leaves of Grass*: *Comprehensive Reader's Edition*, 714.

34. Cf. especially "Nature."

35. See p. 69.

36. *Leaves of Grass*: *Comprehensive Reader's Edition*, 739.

37. *Ibid.*, 745.

38. *Walt Whitman's Poems*, ed. G. W. Allen and C. T. Davis (New York, 1955), 243–248.

39. Fraser, "The Ritual of Death and Resurrection," *Golden Bough*, 692 ff.

40. See p. 127.

41. *Leaves of Grass*: *Comprehensive Reader's Edition*, 421.

42. Roger Asselineau, *The Evolution of Walt Whitman*: *The Creation of a Book* (Harvard University Press, 1962), 101.

Selected Bibliography

CHECK LIST OF EDITIONS PREPARED BY WHITMAN

Leaves of Grass. [First Edition.] Brooklyn, N.Y., 1855. 95 pp.
Leaves of Grass. [Second Edition.] Brooklyn, N.Y., 1856. 384 pp.
Leaves of Grass. [Third Edition.] Boston: Thayer and Eldridge, 1860–61. 456 pp.
Drum-Taps. New York, 1865. 72 pp.
Drum-Taps and *Sequel to Drum-Taps. New York,* N.Y., 1865. 72+24 pp.
Leaves of Grass. [Fourth Edition.] New York, N.Y., 1867. 338 pp.
Leaves of Grass. [Fifth Edition.] Washington, D.C., 1871. 384 pp.
After All Not to Create Only. Boston, 1871. 24 pp.
Democratic Vistas. Washington, D.C., 1871. 84 pp.
Passage to India. Washington, 1871. 120 pp.
As a Strong Bird on Pinions Free and Other Poems. Washington, 1872. 14 pp.
Memoranda During the War. Camden, N.J.,1875–76. 68 pp.
Leaves of Grass. [Sixth Edition.] Camden, N.J., 1876. 384 pp.
Two Rivulets, including *Democratic Vistas, Centennial Songs,* and *Passage to India.* [Companion volume to 1876 *Leaves of Grass.*] Camden, N.J., 1876. 352 pp.
Leaves of Grass. [Seventh Edition.] Boston: James R. Osgood and Co., 1881–82. 382 pp. (Reprinted in Philadelphia by Rees Welsh and Co. in 1882 and thereafter by David McKay.)
Specimen Days and Collect. Philadelphia: Rees Welsh and Co., 1882–83. 374 pp. (Reprinted by David McKay, 1882–83.)
November Boughs. Philadelphia: David McKay, 1888. 140 pp.
Complete Poems and Prose of Walt Whitman, 1855-1888. [Eighth Edition of *Leaves of Grass.*] Philadelphia: published by the author, 1888. 382+374 pp.
Leaves of Grass. With "Sands at Seventy" [first annex to *Leaves of Grass*] and "A Backward Glance O'er Travel'd Roads." [Eighth Edition text.] Philadelphia, 1889. 404+18 pp.
Good-Bye My Fancy. [Second annex to *Leaves of Grass.*] Philadelphia: David McKay, 1891. 66 pp.
Leaves of Grass. [Ninth Edition.] Philadelphia: David McKay, 1891–92. 438 pp.

224

COLLECTED WRITINGS

Complete Prose Works. Philadelphia: David McKay, 1892. 522 pp. (Bound as companion volume to 1891–92 *Leaves.*)

The Complete Writings of Walt Whitman. Issued under the editorial supervision of the Literary Executors. New York and London: G. P. Putnam's Sons, 1902. 10 vols. (Not complete.)

Under the general editorship of Gay Wilson Allen and Sculley Bradley the New York University Press is attempting to publish a complete, definitive edition of *The Collected Writings of Walt Whitman.* Published:

The Early Poems and the Fiction, ed. Thomas L. Brasher, 1963. 352 pp.

Prose Works 1892: Volume I, *Specimen Days,* ed. Floyd Stovall, 1963. 358 pp.

Prose Works 1892: Volume II, *Collect and Other Prose,* ed. Floyd Stovall, 1963. pp. 360–803.

Leaves of Grass: Comprehensive Reader's Edition, ed. Harold W. Blodgett and Sculley Bradley, 1965. 768 pp. (Includes Rejected and Unpublished Poems—and some prefaces.)

The Correspondence (1842–1892), ed. Edwin H. Miller, 1961–69. 5 volumes [all known letters from 1842 to 1892].

In preparation (to be published in 1970–72):

A Variorum Edition of Leaves of Grass, ed. Sculley Bradley and Harold W. Blodgett

Journalism, ed. Herbert Bergman and William White.

Notebooks, Diaries, Miscellany, ed. Edward F. Grier and William White

Bibliography of Publications of Walt Whitman, compiled by William White

BIOGRAPHY AND CRITICISM

Adams, Richard P. "Whitman's 'Lilacs' and the Tradition of Pastoral Elegy," *PMLA,* LXXII, 449–487 (June 1957).

Allen, Gay Wilson. *The Solitary Singer: A Critical Biography of Walt Whitman.* New York: Macmillan, 1955; New York University Press, 1967.

————, ed. *Walt Whitman Abroad:* Critical Essays from Germany, Scandinavia, France, Russia, Italy, Spain, Latin America, Israel, Japan and India. Syracuse, N.Y.: Syracuse University Press, 1955.

————. *Walt Whitman as Man, Poet, and Legend*. With a Check List of Whitman Publications 1945–1960, by Evie Allison Allen. Carbondale, Ill.: Southern Illinois University Press, 1961.

————. *Walt Whitman* [brief biography with over 70 illustrations and selected criticism]. Detroit: Wayne State University Press, 1969.

———— and Charles T. Davis. *Walt Whitman's Poems: Selections with Critical Aids*. New York: New York University Press, 1955.

Asselineau, Roger. *The Evolution of Walt Whitman: The Development of a Personality*. Cambridge, Mass.: Harvard University Press, 1960.

————. *The Evolution of Walt Whitman: The Creation of a Book*. Cambridge, Mass.: Harvard University Press, 1962.

Beaver, Joseph. *Walt Whitman, Poet of Science*. New York: King's Crown Press, 1951.

Bowers, Fredson, ed. *Whitman's Manuscripts: Leaves of Grass* (1860). [Edition of manuscripts with bibliographical and critical interpretations showing growth of third edition.] Chicago: University of Chicago Press, 1955.

Bradley, Sculley. "The Fundamental Metrical Principle in Whitman's Poetry," *American Poetry*, X, 437–459 (January 1939).

Carpenter, Frederic I. "Walt Whitman's Eidólon," in *American Literature and the Dream*. New York: Philosophical Library, 1955.

Catel, Jean. *Rythme et langage dans la 1re édition des "Leaves of Grass"* (1855). Paris, [1930].

Chari, V. K. *Walt Whitman in the Light of Vedantic Mysticism*. Lincoln, Neb.: University of Nebraska Press, 1964.

Chase, Richard. *Walt Whitman Reconsidered*. New York: Sloane, 1955.

Coffman, Stanley K. " 'Crossing Brooklyn Ferry': A Note on the Catalogue Technique in Whitman's Poetry," *Modern Philology*, LI, 225–232 (May 1954).

Cowley, Malcolm. Introduction to *Walt Whitman's Leaves of Grass: The First (1855) Edition*. New York: Viking Press, 1959.

Daiches, David. "Walt Whitman as Innovator," in *The Young Rebel in American Literature*, ed. Carl Bode. London: Heinemann, 1959.

————. "Walt Whitman: Impressionist Prophet," in *Leaves of Grass One Hundred Years After*, ed. Milton Hindus. Palo Alto: Stanford University Press, 1955.

————. "The Philosopher," in *Walt Whitman: Man, Poet, Philosopher: Three Lectures* . . . Washington, D.C.: Library of Congress, 1955.

Faner, Robert D. *Walt Whitman and Opera*. Philadelphia: University of Pennsylvania Press, 1951.

Fiedler, Leslie. "Images of Walt Whitman," in *Leaves of Grass One Hundred Years After*, ed. Milton Hindus. Palo Alto: Stanford University Press, 1955.

Gargano, James W. "Technique in 'Crossing Brooklyn Ferry': The Everlasting Moment," *Journal of English and Germanic Philology*, LXII, 262–269 (April 1963).

Goodale, David. "Some of Walt Whitman's Borrowings," *American Literature*, X, 202–213 (May 1938).

Holloway, Emory. *Whitman: An Interpretation in Narrative*. New York: Knopf, 1926.

Hungerford, Edward. "Walt Whitman and His Chart of Bumps," *American Literature*, II, 350–384 (January 1931).

Jannaccone, P. *La Poesia di Walt Whitman e l'evoluzione delle forme ritmiche*. Torino: Roux Frassati e C° Editori, 1898.

Jarrell, Randall. "Some Lines from Whitman," in *Poetry and the Age*. New York: Knopf, 1953.

Krouse, Sydney J. "Whitman, Music, and *Proud Music of the Storm*," *PMLA*, LXXII, 705–721 (September 1957).

Lawrence, D. H. *Studies in Classic American Literature*. New York: Boni & Liveright, 1923. Chapter 12: "Whitman."

Lewis, R. W. B. "Walt Whitman: Always Going Out and Coming In," in *Trials of the Word: Essays in American Literature and the Humanistic Tradition*. New Haven: Yale University Press, 1965.

Lynen, John F. *The Design of the Present: Essays on Time and Form in American Literature*. New Haven: Yale University Press, 1969.

Marx, Leo. "The Vernacular Tradition in American Literature," in *Studies in American Culture: Dominant Ideas and Images*, ed. Joseph J. Kwiat and Mary C. Turpie. Minneapolis: University of Minnesota Press, 1960.

Miller, Edwin H. *Walt Whitman's Poetry: A Psychological Journey*. New York: New York University Press, 1969.

Miller, James E., Jr. *A Critical Guide to Leaves of Grass*. Chicago: University of Chicago Press, 1957.

————, Karl Shapiro, and Bernice Slote. *Start with the Sun: Studies in Cosmic Poetry*. Lincoln: University of Nebraska Press, 1960.

Musgrove, S. *T. S. Eliot and Walt Whitman*. New York: Columbia University Press, 1953.

Nambiar, O. K. *Walt Whitman and Yoga*. Bangalore, India: Jevan Publications, 1966.

Paine, Gregory. "The Literary Relations of Whitman and Carlyle with Special Reference to their Contrasting Views of Democracy," *Studies in Philology*, XXXVI, 550–563 (July 1939).

Pearce, Roy Harvey. *The Continuity of American Poetry*. Princeton: Princeton University Press, 1961.

Pollak, Georgiana. "The Relationship of Music to 'Leaves of Grass,'" *College English*, XV, 384–394 (April 1954).

Pongs, Herman. "Walt Whitman and Stefan George," in *Walt Whitman Abroad*, ed. Gay Wilson Allen. Syracuse, N.Y.: Syracuse University Press, 1955.

Santayana, George. "The Poetry of Barbarism," in *Interpretations of Poetry and Religion*. New York: Scribners, 1900.

Schuman, Detlev W. "Enumerative Style and Its Significance in Whitman, Rilke, Werfel," *Modern Language Quarterly*, III, 171–204 (June 1942).

Sixbey, George L. " 'Chanting the Square Deific'—A Study in Whitman's Religion," *American Literature*, IX, 171–195 (May 1937).

Spiegelman, Julia. "Walt Whitman and Music," *South Atlantic Quarterly*, XLI, 167–176 (April 1942).

Spitzer, Leo. "*Explication de Texte* Applied to Walt Whitman's Poem 'Out of the Cradle Endlessly Rocking,'" *ELH: A Journal of English Literary History*, XVI, 229–249 (September 1949).

Stovall, Floyd. *American Idealism*. Norman: University of Oklahoma Press, 1943.

Swayne, Mattie. "Whitman's Catalogue Rhetoric," *University of Texas Studies in English*, XXI, 162–178 (1941).

Triggs, Oscar Lovell. "The Growth of 'Leaves of Grass,'" in *The Complete Writings of Walt Whitman*, Camden Edition, ed. Richard Maurice Bucke, Thomas B. Harned, and Horace L. Traubel. New York and London: G. P. Putnam's Sons, 1902. 10 Vols.

Van Doren, Mark. "The Poet," in *Walt Whitman: Man, Poet, Philosopher: Three Lectures* ... Washington, D.C.: Library of Congress, 1955.

Weathers, Willie T. "Whitman's Poetic Translations of His 1855 Preface," *American Literature*, XIX, 21–40 (March 1947).

Ware, Lois. "Poetic Conventions in *Leaves of Grass*," *Studies in Philology*, XXVI, 47–57 (January 1929).

Wendell, Barrett. *A Literary History of America*. New York: Scribners, 1900.

Williams, William Carlos. "An Essay on *Leaves of Grass*," in *Leaves of Grass One Hundred Years After*, ed. Milton Hindus. Palo Alto: Stanford University Press, 1955.

INDEX